How to Set Up and Run Effective Employee Suggestion Schemes

How to Set Up and Run Effective Employee Suggestion Schemes

Second Edition

Paul I Slee Smith

Published in association with
British Institute of Management

First published in 1981 by
British Institute of Management Foundation.

This new edition published in 1989 by
Kogan Page Limited, 120 Pentonville Road, London N1 9JN
in association with British Institute of Management,
Management House, Cottingham Road, Corby, Northants NN17 1TT.

Typeset by J&L Composition Ltd, Filey, North Yorkshire.
Printed and bound in Great Britain by Billing & Sons Ltd, Worcester

British Library Cataloguing in Publication Data
Smith, Paul I. Slee, (Paul Ignatius Slee)
   How to set up and run effective employee
   suggestion schemes. 2nd ed
   1. Organisations. Personnel suggestion
   schemes
   I. Title   II. Smith, Paul I. Slee
   (Paul Ignatius Slee). Employee suggestion
   schemes
   658.3'15

   ISBN 1-85091-803-1

Contents

List of Figures

Acknowledgements

Abbey National Building Society; Aktiebolaget Volvo, Goteborg, Sweden; American Telephone & Telegraph Company; AT & T (UK) Limited; Bayer-Vorschlagwesens; Boeing Aerospace Company; British Airways; British Rail, York; British Telecom; Bureau of Business Practice, United States; Cadbury Limited; Canadian Treasury Board (Incentive Award Board); The Chase Manhatten Bank; Chloride Group; Civil Service Department; Confederation of British Industries; Connecticut General Life Insurance Company; Cossor Electronics Limited; Courtaulds Limited; Cummins Engine Company Inc; Deutsches Institut für Betriebswirtschaft; Dow Chemical Company Limited; Eastman Kodak; E I Du Pont de Nemours Company; Firestone Tyre and Rubber Limited; Ford Motor Company Limited; General Motors Corporation; Hoechst Aktiengesellschaft; Hoover Limited; Hotpoint Limited; Imperial Chemical Industries Limited; The Industrial Society; Inland Revenue; International Business Machines Corporation; International Computers Limited; Kalamazoo Limited; Kodak Limited; Lloyds Bank; Marconi Underwater Systems Limited; Marks & Spencer plc; Mitsubishi Corporation; National Association of Suggestion Systems; National Cash Register Company; National Westminster Bank; Nippon Electric Company; Norwich Union; Pearl Assurance Company Limited; Pedigree Petfoods; Perkins Engines Limited; Philips Data Systems; Philips Petroleum Company Limited; Pilkington Brothers Limited; Prudential Corporation; RCA; Dr Vincent G Reuter Arizona University, United States; Rolls-Royce Limited; Saab-Scania, Sweden; Standard Telephones & Cables Limited; Texas Instruments; Thames Water Ideas Group; Toyota Motor Company; Trustee Saving Bank; UKAE Atomic Energy Establishment, Winfrith; United Airways; United States Office of Personnel Management; Vauxhall Motors Limited; Veba Aktiengesellschaft; W D & H O Wills Limited; Woolwich Equitable Building Society.

Introduction

Since the idea of a suggestion scheme (or programme as it is often known) was first thought of over a hundred years ago, management has become increasingly aware of the rich potential for good constructive ideas that exists in employees' on-the-job experience. The basic concept of Alfred Krupp's original plan has altered little in essentials since those early days in Essen. Its simplicity appeals to present-day industry which has become bigger and more complex, with the result that management is out of direct touch with the actual working process and has become more remote from the workforce.

Suggestion schemes are to be found the world over wherever there is work to be done and improvements are welcomed in industry and commerce. In the United States there is a thriving national body, the National Association of Suggestion Schemes (NASS) supporting 2,000 formal schemes or systems and another 2,000 motivational programmes. In West Germany suggestion schemes are abundant, particularly in the chemical, electronics, steel and engineering industries. The Netherlands and Sweden have possibly the best track record with Volvo and Saab leading the field, and Philips in Holland also has an extremely active scheme, well supported by its 364,000 employees. The United Kingdom Association of Suggestion Schemes (UKASS) was formed in 1987 and today 350 British companies and organisations participate in suggestion schemes producing savings that exceed £35 million.

Suggestion schemes have great flexibility and can be readily adapted to meet all kinds of working conditions and varying economic conditions. They are able to satisfy the exacting requirements of knowledge-intensive industries, such as computers and micro-electronics, and the more traditional industries now struggling hard to meet intense competition from quality and price-conscious foreign manufacturers. It is not only in times of prosperity that suggestion schemes are able to make significant contributions to the profitability of a company, but also in times of recession when there is a pressing need to improve efficiency and build up sales on quality improvements.

It is difficult to isolate the common factors responsible for the survival and eventual prosperity of a company during a recession, but it is generally agreed that two of the most important are the development of new products and the initiation of new ideas for increasing efficiency and improving quality. Too often when trading conditions are tough there is a temptation to cut development and make economies in what are sometimes termed fringe activities, such as suggestion schemes. Happily the temptation to do this is resisted by some of the more forward-looking companies.

Historians remind us that it was the development of the factory system during the Industrial Revolution that largely destroyed the personal bond between employer and employee and whilst it would be absurd to claim that any suggestion scheme could do much to restore that bond, at least it helps to identify the worker with the progress of the company, provides an acceptable way of improving the employer–employee relationship and of encouraging workers to think creatively about their job. By encouraging the employee to contribute ideas for improvement, a new incentive is given to him and his attitude to work undergoes a change for the better. In many western countries there has been a marked deterioration in people's attitude to work over the last decade. It is reported that in American industry today only one in four workers look to their employment as a source of fulfilment, whereas in Japan three out of four workers are imbued with a sense of mission and enjoy their work, often under conditions grossly inferior to those found in the average American factory.

When Professor Herzberg presented his motivation-hygiene theory in the late 1960s, he drew attention to the fact that while industry had satisfied man's outer wants with those material things necessary for the good life, it had lost sight of the inner needs necessary for man's creative survival. The truth of this is becoming increasingly evident every year and it is now being realised that without a fundamental change in man's attitude to work there can be no upsurge in productivity. Although the suggestion scheme is only one of a number of motivational programmes favoured by the more progressive companies, it ranks as the most satisfying both in terms of the tangible benefits which accrue from ideas of substance and of intangible rewards, such as individual recognition and the opportunity to take an active part in problem solving and decision making. Employee participation in solving production problems is now being recognised as a prime factor in motivating employee interest in the progress of the

company. There are, of course, some organisations where suggestions from employees evolve freely and naturally without resort to
a suggestion scheme and its award system; in Japanese industry
rewards for money-saving ideas are mostly psychological and in
some firms an original proposal put forward by a worker is only
rewarded with a ballpoint pen. However, the experience in western industry would seem to confirm the view that even where
workers' ideas come spontaneously, a well-run suggestion scheme
plays a welcome reinforcing role. Although most managements
now accept the idea of greater employee participation in theory,
they often fail to apply it in practice. An efficient, management-
supported suggestion scheme can be an exercise in employee
participation in solving production problems.

This book is an attempt to explain why suggestion schemes are
so important not only in providing a rich harvest of money-saving
ideas but in developing employee involvement and joint problem
solving. By encouraging more understanding and involvement in
the business, more joint problem solving and more joint decision
making at the lowest level possible, a well-run scheme can help to
create a sense of belonging to the team – the organisation.

1. The Development of Suggestion Schemes

The first practical attempt to encourage employees to submit ideas for improvements by offering them small monetary rewards was made by Alfred Krupp at his steel works in Essen in 1867. In his book, *General Regulativ*, written in 1872 when he retired, Krupp attempted to set out the rights and duties of his employees: 'If you have any ideas for improvements, inventions and innovations, or doubts about the usefulness of established methods, these should be brought to the notice of your immediate superiors who will then make them known to the management for checking.'

In Britain the first suggestion scheme was introduced in 1880 at the Dumbarton shipyard of William Denny and Brothers and a few years later a somewhat similar scheme was in operation at Barr and Stroud's engineering works in Glasgow. The early years of the twentieth century witnessed a number of suggestion schemes being tried out in British industry, the most notable one being sponsored by George Cadbury (Junior) at the Bourneville chocolate works in 1904 as a result of a visit he paid to the National Cash Register Company in America, which was running a highly successful scheme. Awards were based on a percentage of the estimated savings to the company during the first year of operation; up to 1939 the largest award paid was £250 awarded to a man in 1937–38 for economies in material. There is no doubt that the Cadbury scheme proved very popular: from its inception in 1905 to its wartime suspension in 1939, 60,000 ideas were received from women employees and 81,000 from men. Women earned awards totalling £3,255 and men £9,577. The largest award was £100 to a man and £20 to a woman. The exact percentage of the awards based on savings to the company was never stated. (Sadly, the Cadbury scheme is no longer in existence, as in 1986 it was judged to be uneconomical.)

Another early scheme, started in 1908, is still running at Kalamazoo in Birmingham. Their example was followed by a number of other famous companies, such as Lucas in 1921; IBM (UK) Ltd in 1928, following their parent company in the United States; Imperial Chemical Industries throughout its various divisions in 1930, and Vauxhall Motors in 1940. However, the majority of those running today came into existence after the Second World War.

In 1987 the United Kingdom Association of Suggestion Schemes (UKASS), was formed due largely to the enterprise of the Industrial Society. Today there are 350 British companies and organisations participating in suggestion schemes producing savings of £35 million with awards to suggestors totalling £5 million. There is abundant evidence of a great revival of interest in suggestion schemes and a new professional approach has been made by new companies anxious to harness the creativity and talent of their employees.

Suggestion systems in the United States

In the United States there are about 2,000 formal suggestion systems and possibly an equal number of motivational programmes of one form or another that embody suggestion plans. There is a very active National Association of Suggestion Systems (NASS) with headquarters in Chicago. Its 1,000 members include the largest and most powerful companies in the country with a total of eleven million employees. According to NASS its members process over a million suggestions a year, a quarter of them being adopted for implementation. Awards paid out to employees for money-saving ideas in 1978 amounted to $42,379,976, the average award being $132.74. The highest individual award paid out during that year was $75,000. From the employer's angle it is of interest to note that the average net saving per adoption was $1,476.50.

In the United States 'knowledge-intensive' industries showed the highest participation rate and 'resource-intensive' industries the lowest. Indicative of the importance attached to suggestion systems in America is the fact that there is a highly successful Federal Incentive Awards Program which in 1979 paid out $3,888,190 in awards to federal employees. Measurable benefits to the government amounted to $147,721,814 with average benefits running at $3,520 and average awards $123.10.

Suggestions systems in Europe

West Germany takes the lead in Europe with most of the larger companies having suggestion schemes. During the last ten years the engineering workforce has produced ideas for improvement at the rate of 160 per thousand employees. Germany's interest in such schemes is hardly surprising in view of the country's long tradition of successful suggestion plans. In 1967 anniversary celebrations were held throughout many sections of German industry to mark a hundred years of suggestion systems in Germany. The chemical industry is particularly prominent in promoting suggestion systems and firms like Hoechst and Bayer attach great importance to workers' ideas for improvements, particularly in the realms of safety. Judged by American and British standards, German awards for workers' suggestions are not particularly generous; at the start of the suggestion system at the Hoechst works in 1930, a foreman in the azo dye plant was awarded RM 150 (equivalent to about DM 1,800 today) for a valuable idea which led to greater ease of manufacture. All suggestion plans in German industry are actively promoted by major advertising campaigns, including posters, leaflets, works newspapers and other publications, as well as lotteries for suggestion award winners, special exhibitions featuring workers' ideas and social functions at which award winners are feted by management. In 1971, Hoechst organised an 'Ideas Olympics' in which special recognition was given to employees who submitted more than one suggestion. An important aspect of the German suggestion system is that the unions give the idea their full support and encourage their members to participate.

Other countries in Europe follow the same general pattern as in the United Kingdom, most of the leading companies having suggestion schemes. The Industrial Society puts the number at about 500 schemes currently on offer in the UK. It is interesting to note that one of the first suggestion schemes was started in a Belgian coal mining company at the end of the nineteenth century. The Netherlands and Scandinavian countries have probably the best track record when it comes to suggestion systems, eg Philips in Holland, Volvo and Saab in Sweden. All employees at Volvo, irrespective of status and responsibility, are free to join the scheme and participate in cash awards. In 1979 the company made its highest award, $18,200, to a member of its office staff (engine division) for an outstanding innovative suggestion (see Table 1).

Table 1 Suggestions activities within the Volvo Group of Companies, 1979

| | Calculated for the total number of companies | | |
	Workers	Salaried employees	Total
Number of employees	28,694	13,146	41,840
Number of suggestions	4,439	756	5,195
Average per 100 employees	15	6	12
Number of suggestions considered	4,265	695	4,962
Number of suggestions compensated	1,484	135	1,619
Compensated as % of considered	35	19	33
Total compensation in dollars	411,000	66,000	477,000
Average dollar compensation per suggestion	275	490	295
Highest amount for one suggestion	13,700	18,200	

The USSR and Eastern Europe

Managements in Soviet factories are primarily concerned with meeting the targets set by their five-year plans, and workers are given every encouragement to exceed production norms. Innovations, inventions and improvements are rewarded by bonuses, which can be substantial: extra salary, extra vacational facilities at Black Sea and Baltic resorts, privileged purchasing facilities for consumer goods in short supply, and special opportunities for advancement. Moral incentives such as titles, pennants, honours, places on boards of honour, special citations are extra inducements.

Japan

In Japan a number of the large companies have employee suggestion schemes run more or less on western lines except that awards are usually much smaller than those paid out in Britain or America, greater emphasis being given to personal recognition – a lapel button may be the only visible sign of an award. Throughout Japanese industry there is close co-operation between management and employees, especially when making plans for future investment and expansion. Plans and projects are originally made at the bottom levels and then sent to the top for final decisions, whereas in western companies the standard procedure is for plans to be made at top level and sent down to lower levels to be put into practice. Most of the projects of the giant Mitsubishi Company are planned at section level and then sent up the company ladder for decision making. Quality circle activities for blue and white-collar workers play an increasingly important role in both industrial and commercial concerns, and are claimed to be responsible for high productivity and the training of an elite labour force that is quality conscious. At Nippon Kokan KK there are 8,000 workers in 1,480 circles, and in 1979 these accounted for more than $86 million in cost savings to the company. Nippon Electric Company's Fuchu plant doubled productivity in three years due largely to the input of workers' ideas for improvement.

2. Advantages of Suggestion Schemes

From a hard-nosed business angle, it might appear that the sole objective of a suggestion scheme is to make available to the employer a continuous supply of useful ideas that will enable him to increase productivity, cut costs, eliminate waste, save energy, etc, all of which will produce tangible savings that will help to make him more competitive. There is no doubt that these tangible results are important and, indeed, can contribute substantially to the success of a business. However, there are other less tangible advantages to be gained from a suggestion scheme which could be of greater significance than actual savings to the employer and awards to the employee.

One of the more important of these is the ability of the scheme to influence the attitude of the employee towards change. It is recognised that change, because it threatens security, has a disturbing effect on people and that is why they tend to resist it, but if workers are encouraged to put forward their own ideas for improvements which represent changes in working methods, they tend to become more receptive to changes introduced by management. In the fiercely competitive world of modern business change is inevitable, and the only way to dispel some of the natural fears and worries of employees faced with changes in their jobs is for management to prepare the ground beforehand by allowing them time to reorientate themselves to the new conditions. In Japanese industry, where there is an insatiable hunger for technological change that will increase competitiveness, the greatest care is taken to see that no changes are made until all the people involved agree.

Increase profitability

In 1986 some 800 Austin Rover employees received awards for money-saving ideas that amounted to £290,000. The company processes some 8,000 suggestions every year and pays out awards based on 20 % of the proven net savings over the year with a minimum pay-out of £15 and a maximum of £5,000 plus a new car if the idea saves the company £150,000. A foreman at British Steel's

Whitehead plant in Newport won the overall trophy for the 1988 Best Suggestion with his idea of replacing the present motorway safety barriers made of welded steel sections with one-piece barriers made of steel. The new product was cheaper to make and more effective in action. For this idea the man was awarded the coveted £1,200 Works Award, plus a new motor car and two tickets to travel to the United States.

The Lucas suggestion scheme launched in 1921 has now generated 2 million suggestions; during 1987 some 6,000 were submitted from 400 UK Lucas factories. Of these, 50 per cent were adopted – with £157,000 paid out in cash awards to employees. In 1987 an employee at the company's Girling brake factory was paid £1,000 for a novel idea to prevent incorrect assembly of wheel-brake cylinders and £1,500 was handed to another worker for an easier and cheaper method of changing contaminated filter pads.

In 1987, Vauxhall Motors staff received awards for bright ideas totalling £230,568 for 4,000 suggestions. Since the scheme was first founded in 1942, as a wartime measure, over £1,500,000 has been paid out in awards.

In June 1987, which seemed a very good month for awards, £12,000 was paid out to eight men in three divisions of ICI for cost-saving ideas. One of the largest cash awards, £23,000, was made in 1987 to a member of staff working for Shell UK at Ellesmere Port. The British Telecom scheme has produced savings of £1.5 million since its launch in 1984.

All these examples attest to a growing awareness of the value of suggestion schemes within British industry – as a means of increasing profit *and* worker participation. However, a suggestion scheme cannot hope to produce instant savings that cover costs – but within a year or so a scheme should be able to show a profit.

This is the experience of the Volvo Group of Companies. When their scheme was launched, the savings from the first year's operations were disappointing and scarcely paid administrative costs. Yet within the second year the benefits to the company more than satisfied the accountants and, indeed, many of the improvements introduced as a result of workers' suggestions produced long-term savings that have not yet been fully estimated. Saab-Scania, another famous Swedish firm, reports that it receives a threefold return on expenditure and regards the operation as a sound investment. German firms like Bayer, Hoechst and the Veba organisation also stress the economic advantages of their suggestion programmes which are now accepted throughout their factories as an integral part of industrial life.

In the United States the majority of the companies running suggestion systems maintain that they yield a profit, both as regards actual savings due to the improvements introduced and intangible benefits, such as individual recognition, better morale and improved working conditions. In a survey carried out by the National Association of Suggestion Systems covering more than a thousand suggestion programmes, it was shown that on average five dollars was realised in tangible net cost savings for each dollar spent on running the scheme. Total first-year savings to American employers with suggestion plans of one kind or another were estimated by NASS to be $481 million, of which nearly $35 million was paid out to employees. In 1979 Philips Petroleum Company obtained tangible savings from employee suggestions to the value of $4.9 million and gave out $461,080 in awards to workers. Of these savings, Philips say that $813,520 were 'one-time savings', the remainder were expected to have at least a three-year life. Although the Philips suggestion system cost the company $1,151,000 in 1979, it yields a four-to-one return.

Boeing Aerospace Company's suggestion system showed a substantial increase in the first quarter of 1980 as the following figures show:

Year	Suggestions received (1st quarter only)	Cost savings (1st quarter only)
1977	515	$84,242
1978	397	$368,463
1979	606	$563,455
1980	917	$845,327

In the first quarter of 1980 participation reflected an increase of 66% over a similar period in 1979. (The majority of these increased levels were from BAC Manufacturing and BAC Electronic Support Division.) Monetary awards amounting to $79,926 were paid during the first quarter of 1980 compared with $41,319 during the first quarter of 1979. A comparison with other suggestion systems in the Seattle area indicates that the company's system has the highest dollar return on awards given:

Location	Awards	Savings	Return
Renton	$528,555	$4,805,591	9.09:1
Everett	$335,617	$2,527,345	7.53:1
Auburn	$585,095	$6,620,040	11.32:1
BAC	$171,515	$2,099,148	12.24:1

Record savings were also obtained by the Firestone Company, and in 1979 these amounted to $3,884,063. Some 42,395 suggestions were submitted by employees and 7,766 adopted. What is particularly interesting about Firestone is that all the international plants were successful in attracting record numbers of suggestions, earning the company $488,428 in savings during the fiscal year 1978–79.

In Canada, most of the big corporations running suggestion systems report satisfactory returns. The Public Service of Canada, responsible for the administration of employee incentive programmes throughout the Federal Government, stated in their Annual Report for 1978–79 that employee suggestions adopted for use in the various departments of government reduced expenditure by $5,453,018. Suggestion programmes, which were authorised in the United States Federal Government in 1954, also report very satisfactory savings: during the 1979 fiscal year the army produced suggestion benefits exceeding $35 million for the thirteenth consecutive year; the airforce reported benefits exceeding $20 million, and the navy $10 million. The National Security Agency, with benefits exceeding $100 million, affords one of the best examples of the efficacy of the government-sponsored scheme.

It is misleading to quote first-year savings from suggestions as indicative of the returns to the employer, as the benefits from an adopted suggestion are often spread over several years. Three years' savings represent an average figure, although it is known that many suggestions are still producing savings after ten years. Professor Vincent G Reuter, Professor of Management Studies at Arizona University, who has made a special study of the economics of suggestion plans, maintains that after allowing for all administrative costs as well as awards, most schemes provide a monetary return of two to eight times the running cost.

With some suggestions the implementation costs may be heavy, but these can be spread over the expected life of the suggestion: by dividing the cost of implementation by the maximum life years of the suggestion, perhaps only one-third or one-fifth of the cost is charged against the suggestion in any one year.

On the other hand, many suggestions involve practically no implementation costs, merely a change in standard procedure. A British Airways Concorde co-pilot devised a technique for flying Concorde accurately round an arrival circuit at Heathrow using the aircraft's own navigation system as opposed to flying under Air Traffic Control's radar system. This simple change in procedure which involved no extra equipment, enabled the airliner to obtain an inbound routing shorter in track mileage and different from the ones used by subsonic aircraft, and on which the plane was able to keep up its speed. This simple idea, which won the pilot British Airways' top award of £5,000, will save the company more than a million kilograms of aviation fuel a year. Another example of a money-saving idea that cost nothing to implement was put forward by an American airline pilot some years ago. He saved his firm $458,500 in the first year simply by moving cargo so as to shift the airliner's centre of gravity. His award from United Airlines was a record $45,850.

Another British Airways employee, an electrician at Heathrow Airport, was awarded £5,000 for a brilliant idea that concerned the provision of an early-warning system for solving problems on secondary air doors on the Concorde. A design change to the circuitry put forward by the BA employee was successful in achieving savings of £160,000, as well as preventing flight turn back, fuel jettison and inconvenience to passengers.

Today, increasing emphasis is being placed on clerical work where ideas which will reduce costs, improve service, prevent waste, save time, improve methods, combine forms, save supplies and improve work-flow are greatly in demand by progressive managements. In 1974, two officers of the Inland Revenue suggested that the organisation should install turn-o-matic machines in their offices to deal with callers in strict rotation and avoid queueing. The award of £300 was then a record.

In the commercial field, such as insurance, some of the largest companies in the United States, eg Connecticut General Life Insurance, find that employees' ideas for improvements in office procedure or field work can often give a sharper edge to their competitive position. This becomes evident when one looks at the awards given to employees for ideas of substance. Connecticut General Life base their awards on 25% of the first year's net savings, with a top figure of $25,000.

The real value of a suggestion in terms of net savings cannot always be accurately assessed as some improvements may offer a diversity of applications; for instance in a large company with several manufacturing plants, some of them abroad, a suggestion adopted and implemented in one works may be taken up by another factory and put to work to earn more money. By widening the field of applications for a worker's idea, the company stands to increase its savings quite substantially and, of course, the suggestor's award is also increased.

There is no escaping the fact that suggestion schemes are expensive. Apart from employing extra staff to do the paperwork there are indirect costs involved in investigating the ideas put forward by employees. However, when all the sums have been done, experience gained by hard-headed American businessmen shows that the average net saving per adoption worked out at $5,554 in 1986, and the net savings per 100 eligible employees at $19,759. The United Kingdom Suggestion Schemes' average award is £201 and this generates an average saving of £850. Of greater significance than trying to balance the books is the hidden benefit in terms of worker participation. When an employee puts forward a bright idea that contributes in a small way to the welfare of the firm he or she has the satisfaction of making a personal contribution. Motivation in the company is largely motivation of groups – those employees who take part in a suggestion scheme represent a very important group. Those who think about their job and are encouraged to plan and use their imagination must in the end help to produce a much healthier and happier climate in the workplace. The fact that such a small proportion of ideas win awards – often as low as 4% in some of the large stores – gives no true idea of their intrinsic value.

Experience has shown that frequently an idea for an improvement put forward by one person in a workshop or administrative department triggers off a number of associated ideas from individuals or groups in the same workshop or department. For example, in one government office a suggestion which resulted in a reduction in paper purchases encouraged other workers to submit ideas for making economies in floor space, computer time and the more economical use of shelving.

Improve employee attitudes

Suggestion schemes also improve employees' attitudes by directing their attention to the positive and progressive aspects of their jobs – by helping to boost employee morale and increase job satisfaction. If an employee is unhappy in his job, it is almost certain that this negative attitude will be reflected not only in his job performance but in his relations with other people; for example in a service industry there is a good chance that this negative attitude will become obvious to customers and, perhaps adversely influence business in the long term. Although low employee morale is an intangible force, it can be a powerful one. Experience in many companies has shown that it is often one of the prime reasons for low productivity and frequently paves the way for costly errors. Suggestion programmes can play a useful role in increasing and maintaining high morale. They also act as a useful barometer: when morale is high and a good working relationship exists between management and the workforce, the calibre of suggestions is normally high; whereas if morale is poor, the calibre is low. Provided management runs its business on sound principles and runs its suggestion scheme on the right lines, that is efficiently and fairly, then there is every reason to expect it to be a profitable venture, both for the employer and the employee. As many authorities have said 'A successful suggestion system does not cost – it pays'.

The remote corporate bureaucracies now running some or our great industrial and commercial enterprises have tended to isolate employees from all decision making. Behavioural scientists have for a long time pointed out the dangers of functional specialisation which robs work of all initiative and discourages the enquiring mind. An increasing awareness of the deterioration in the quality of work, and the lowering of standards due to increasing specialisation of tasks, has brought to the fore the pressing need for job enrichment, so as to provide new opportunities for the exercise of a variety of skills. Herzberg reported some years ago that the content of the individual job to a large extent determines workers' motivation. Nowadays, the weight of evidence would seem to support this view, and many workers in the field have proposed changes in the structure of jobs so as to increase the responsibility of individual workers. The most welcome and desirable changes are those that bring variety and challenge to the job, and lessen the risk of a machine wholly dictating both the pace and the nature of work. In many spheres of modern industry the operative carries out relatively simple tasks which, to him, are often meaningless and monotonous, and result in boredom and actual dislike of the job.

According to Pehr Gyllenhammar, President of Volvo, the way out of the modern industrial mismatch is to design jobs for people which give them responsibility and scope, and thus encourage them to do a full day's work because they feel that what they do really matters. Work which demeans people should not be tolerated and wherever mechanisation and technology can be used to eliminate dreary or disagreeable work, then changes should be made to bring about improvements. The Volvo system encourages the worker to introduce improvements based on his own ideas and thereby identify more closely with the job. It has fostered a new approach to work in which acceptance of change and doing the job the most sensible way have become more important than some historical precedent or demarcation practice.

Gyllenhammar did more than diagnose the trouble, he made sure that his diagnosis was translated into action by designing a radically different assembly process for the Volvo car using the now famous 'Volvo Wagon' instead of the traditional conveyor belt, and by dividing his factory at Kalmar into work group areas where specialist teams were able to work under the best possible conditions.

Summary

1. Improves job attitudes by arousing greater interest both in the work and the product.
2. Helps foster higher employee morale.
3. Makes use of constructive ideas of employees and at the same time gives them a tangible share in the benefits.
4. Reduces the tendency for employees to resist change.
5. Encourages co-operation in solving shop-floor problems and joint decision making at the lowest level.
6. Opens up a useful two-way communication between employer and employee.
7. Serves as a management safety valve by offering employees the opportunity to substitute a constructive solution to a problem that might remain an unspoken complaint and irritation.
8. Gives personal recognition to employees with good ideas.

3. Eligibility

General considerations

Industry is hungry for new ways to cut costs and increase productivity. Inflation and other pressures have resulted in higher costs for every raw material, part, product, and service that manufacturers have to buy. Wasted materials and scrap, which at one time were shrugged off as inevitable write-offs, are now recognised as major contributors to high operating costs. There is a growing consciousness that help is urgently needed in solving shop-floor problems and that the most sensible approach is to seek this help from the factory floor itself. So far, problem solving by the workforce has not been taken up very seriously by management in Britain, although there is growing evidence that in other parts of the world it can pay rich dividends.

In Japan, for example, problem solving by the workforce has, for some years now, been taken for granted. Although few western firms are prepared to follow the line of decision making by consensus of opinion as practised by Mitsubishi and other large corporations, there is a feeling that British industry is losing out because it does not make greater use of the rich potential of workers' ideas for improvement.

One of the first problems facing any company that sets up a suggestion scheme is the need to define what types of suggestions will be acceptable under their scheme and which grades of employee will be eligible to take part.

Acceptable suggestions

An idea for an improvement may represent a change in standard practices. It need not be new or original, indeed many excellent suggestions are old ideas adapted to different operations or new situations. The most acceptable suggestions in industry are those that result in improvement of operations and procedures, reduction in costs, savings in energy, material, time and labour. However, suggestions dealing with safety, health, fire and accident prevention, reduction in contamination, quality control, improvements in working conditions, and good housekeeping may all qualify for awards.

The degree of importance, and therefore the awards for ideas in these areas, differs widely from industry to industry and company to company. Those industries that depend heavily on energy and energy-related materials give a special welcome to innovative ideas leading to economies in energy and in many plants workers are being encouraged to think of ideas of saving energy. A number of well-known companies now promote special schemes to whip up the interest of their employees in ways of cutting down on energy requirements both in factories and offices. In the chemical industry a high priority is usually given to safety and health; while in others, such as the production of consumer goods, the attitude often adopted by employers is that safety is adequately covered by government regulations and is primarily the responsibility of the safety officer and outside the scope of a suggestion scheme.

Throughout the manufacturing industries there exists a wide difference of opinion about the merits of certain types of suggestions. For example, in the motor industry ideas for changes in the appearance of the product are not viewed with great enthusiasm, whereas in certain sections of the food industry considerable importance is attached to suggestions for improving the appearance of goods. Quality control is another rather intangible factor which some companies still tend to look upon as outside the normal suggestion scheme; yet in the pharmaceutical industry quality control is regarded as vital and employee suggestions for improving and maintaining it are well rewarded.

Computer systems now provide excellent opportunities for high award suggestions. A data control clerk employed by Perkins Engines earned £1,580 for a paper saving idea. She became concerned about the enormous volume of high-grade, expensive computer paper used in day-to-day operations and started to think of ways to cut this down. Her idea, which was a very simple one, was to eliminate the reference print-out and record the information on magnetic tape. This substitution enabled substantial economies to be made not only in computer listing sheets but in the time required for filing and other activities. The Inland Revenue recently paid £1,200 to a member of their staff who suggested that certain entries on one of their forms need not be totalled in future because computerisation was able to provide the same information, and an employee at their Computer Centre at Shipley won a record high award, £9,000 for a bright idea that improved efficiency.

In any one works, irrespective of the type of manufacture carried out, there are always certain operations that particularly lend themselves to award-winning ideas because of the unique opportunities offered for improvements in techniques and effecting economies in the use of materials. In the motor industry the most regular award winners are generally found in the press room. This is because there is nowhere else in the factory where it is possible to take a closer and more critical look at the bodywork of the vehicle, and to decide where it might be possible to make economies in the use of sheet metal in the production of body and chassis panels. Machining operations also present a rich source of ideas for avoiding tool breakages, reducing wear on cutting tools and methods of re-using worn tools.

The majority of ideas adopted from workers in the engineering-based industries relate to material saving and the avoidance of scrap, the use of quicker methods or deleting unnecessary operations, the use of different methods to give improved appearance or better quality, economies in heating, lighting and other services.

In the chemical and allied industries, special emphasis is placed on the following ideas:

- Improvements in process efficiency, product quality, materials and energy conservation;
- Improvements in working methods and materials handling;
- Improvements in damage avoidance and human safety;
- Improvements in the design of machinery, tools, equipment, etc, so as to increase efficiency;
- Reduction in capital needs for plant and equipment and all stocks of materials.

In commercial and administrative establishments campaigns are directed towards eliminating paperwork, improving and simplifying the design of forms, improving and simplifying clerical methods, improving office practices and routines, and making better use of office aids and equipment. Service industries usually give priority to workers' ideas for improving customer service or helping to achieve broad corporate goals.

The DHSS has been operating a scheme for 40 years. The department employs about 100,000 staff, mostly in 500 local security offices and now receives over 7,000 suggestions every year. Very substantial awards are made for money-saving ideas and throughout the country staff are being encouraged to put forward suggestions for producing new incomes for hospitals and improving the service to patients.

One of the best hospital suggestion schemes the author has come across was at the 800-bed District and General Hospital in Norwich. The management had operated a traditional staff suggestion scheme for some years without any real success but it came to life when someone thought of the novel slogan – 'IVAN IDEA'. The scheme, based on inexpensive gifts and rewards, was stimulated by notices displayed throughout the hospital at specific intervals.

The scheme was an immediate success and produced some 2,500 ideas, a high percentage of which were implemented and produced worthwhile savings. Several national newspapers reported the novel scheme and the local radio and TV channels as well as the local newspaper gave it good coverage.

One idea which emerged from the scheme was to use blue paper towels instead of white ones. This saved the hospital £10,000 a year since blue paper can be made from waste paper. The cost of printing the posters and buying the pens and mugs used as rewards (as well as subsidising some of the raffle prizes) cost £4,000 – so the actual savings to the hospital from this one suggestion amounted to more than twice the cost of running the entire scheme. Although now two years old, IVAN has still plenty of life in him and it is hoped to achieve a target of £90,000 recurring savings to be returned to patient service.

The results of the IVAN IDEA Scheme included:

Administration

- Reducing compliment-slip design from 40 to one;
- Economies in medical records forms;
- Staggered lunch breaks to improve services;
- Cashless pay initiatives;
- Greater emphasis on commercial opportunities;
- Strict control on introducing new forms;
- Re-use of envelopes using adhesive labels.

Clinical areas

- Video entertainment in out-patient areas;
- Economies in central sterile supplies;
- Exchange service for orthopaedic implants;
- Additional canteen/kiosk facility for out-patients.

NORFOLK & NORWICH HOSPITAL

IVAN IDEA SCHEME

Have you an idea that can save money or produce income?

**If so tell your co-ordinator and win a pen, mug
or a chance to win a cash prize.**

Your co-ordinator is . . . .

Figure 1: The 'Ivan Idea' suggestion scheme

Service departments

- Economies in surgical footwear;
- Review of staff uniform requirements;
- Laundry economies;
- Visitors to use staff dining facilities;
- Continental breakfasts six days a week;
- Realistic beverage charges for staff;
- Saturday shoppers' car park.

In listing suggested avenues for ideas, ICI gives this advice to employees: 'Whatever you do, or see being done, remember there must be a better way and better ways make sense and money for you and the company.

In 1980 an energy-saving idea earned an electrician at ICI's Fibre Division at Wilton, Teeside, £1,654. During the comparative quiet of a shutdown he noticed that the main-drive electric motor on a yarn cutter was running, although the cutter was not in use. He would not have heard it if the plant had been operating under normal conditions. 'How could the motor be switched off when the cutter was not in use?' was the question the electrician asked himself. The answer, he found was a timing device to switch off the motor after a predetermined time if the clutch had not been energised. This man's idea produced substantial savings for ICI and was adopted throughout the Fibres Division plants at Wilton.

In the United States some of the big corporations with a high percentage of white-collar workers have organised campaigns to persuade employees to put forward suggestions for reducing turnover, improving morale and improving community relations. At first sight these may seem rather far removed from actual production problems but they may be of the greatest importance to the prosperity and future development of the firm.

Simplicity

Simplicity is usually the keynote of most on-the-job suggestions derived from a close observation of working conditions. For example at one of the Chloride Group factories an operative in the packing department earned for himself an award of £1,164 for a very simple modification to the design of box pallets, which enabled them to be packed higher in greater safety. This idea improved productivity and enabled warehouse space to be used more economically. Another simple modification of equipment which greatly increased efficiency earned a worker in ICI's Agricultural Division a handsome award. By re-arranging the hydraulic ram on a mechanical shovel it proved possible to prolong its life by reducing wear and damage to a minimum.

Extending the life of equipment

Throughout industry increasing attention is being given to ways of lengthening the life of expensive plant and machines to reduce maintenance and replacements. This is where shop-floor experience and ingenuity can pay dividends. Foremen and supervisors are able to play an important role by focusing the attention of workers on specific problems where trouble has been encountered in the past. It is not intended that supervisory staff should attempt to solve these problems themselves. Their function is rather to encourage staff to think around them and come up with possible solutions, some of which could be developed into practical suggestions that would earn them money.

A good example of a money-saving idea to prolong the life of equipment is afforded by a suggestion put forward by a fitter at Courtaulds Aintree works where it was found that the wear and tear on lubricant rollers in the Celon spinning process was responsible for expensive replacements during the year, and the management was looking for ways of cutting costs by prolonging the life of the rollers. The fitter's idea was to grind off the scratches and chips which made rollers unusable and regroove them with a diamond tool. By using this method the factory's engineering workshop was able to cut down substantially on replacement costs.

Production problems masquerading as suggestions

It sometimes happens that production bottle-necks are put forward as suggestions without any real attempt being made to provide solutions. Whilst the normal procedure is to reject these so-called suggestions and remind the originators that they cannot be considered as bona fide suggestions because no attempt is made to provide solutions to the problems that have been outlined, this course of action may not be in the best interests of the company. Management may be blissfully unaware that these production problems exist and, in any case, it is worth encouraging the employee to use his ingenuity in trying to find an answer. Some years ago General Motors introduced a programme which they called ECI or 'Error Cause Identification', using a special four-part form for employees to complete. The purpose of the scheme, which ran alongside the formal suggestion plan, was to encourage workers to draw management's attention to any condition which they believed needed correction. The employee made no attempt to correct the fault, merely pointing out that it existed. The exercise proved to be a great success and aroused wide interest as it provided ready-made goals for observant suggestors. Supervisory staff at General Motors played a leading role in this exercise and in discussions with their staff they sought to bring out some of the day-to-day problems the men had encountered in their work.

Implementation costs

The savings which result from implementing a suggestion have always to be considered against the cost of making the suggestion work. Implementation costs in materials, man-hours, tools or equipment purchased or modified, planning and development time, etc, can mount up to a considerable sum and may, even be more than the actual savings over the first year. However, as indicated in Chapter 2 the saving can usually be made over several years. Not all ideas cost money to implement; for example, productivity in one electronic engineering works was greatly improved by placing jigs, coils and tools at locations which did not interfere with the operation of machines and yet were within easy reach of operators so that many wasteful movements could be eliminated and the distance between work points shortened.

To succeed, suggestions must promise solid improvements, such as saving time, materials or paperwork, simplifying procedures or processes or improving services. Where the benefits derived from implementing a suggestion cannot be measured in money terms, eg quality control, safety, security, eliminating health risks, or environmental improvements, appreciation is usually determined by the degree of impact of the idea and the extent to which it can be applied.

Rules governing acceptability

Experience has shown that sometimes problems arise due to the inability of firms to define clearly the rules governing the acceptability of suggestions. These should be set out as follows:

1. Suggestions should be submitted in a legible manner on the special forms provided by the company.
2. Suggestions shall include:
   a) a specific statement of what is suggested and how it can be accomplished;
   b) a brief statement describing the present methods, practices or problems;
   c) a statement of the savings, improved services, or benefits which will accrue from adoption of the suggestion.
3. Suggestions must also include the suggestor's signature, position, department or workshop, etc, and whether anyone else has a proprietary interest in the idea put forward.

Ideas not generally accepted

1. Suggestions that are part of the ordinary job responsibilities of the suggestor.
2. Information on updating records, instructions, drawings, routings etc.
3. Items normally covered by the maintenance programme or which arise out of minor defects in maintenance or installation, eg painting or re-painting, attention to leaking valves or glands, lagging of pipes and replacement of machine guards, etc.
4. Ideas relating to recreation facilities, vending machines, parking, requisition or purchase of goods in common use.
5. Correction of minor errors on forms or literature and minor changes in design.
6. Modifications to plant or machinery which do not result in any significant increase in productivity but merely add to the operator's convenience or ease of operation.
7. Minor changes or modifications to new equipment, plant or processes within the jointly agreed period of commissioning.
8. All matters governed by contract with others.
9. Improvements or changes in design which infringe existing patents.
10. Ideas which have been thought of before and discarded for various reasons, except those being held for a 'retention period' (see Chapter 6).
11. Suggestions relating to trade union practice, working hours, profit sharing, disclosure of information, job rotation, job enlargement, etc, which are considered outside the scope of the suggestion scheme.
12. Ideas that cannot be implemented at the time of submission because of excessive cost, or limitations of known technology or business methods.
13. Ideas, methods or equipment already under consideration or development. This is a tricky one and it is difficult to make the

suggestor understand the true position. Some kind of encouragement award should be given in recognition of the employee's initiative.

14. Intangibles. Some companies rule out certain intangible suggestions such as housekeeping, amenities, safety, etc, which they consider are outside the scope of the suggestion scheme. The suggestor should be reminded of the rules governing the scheme.

15. Building services including signage.

16. Suggestions which are impractical in their present form, ie the basic idea may be good but the suggestor's proposal for implementation faulty from a technical angle. The suggestor should be advised to seek expert help in developing his idea along practical lines, and then to submit the suggestion again in a revised form.

17. Suggestions that contravene accepted standards of safety or work practices.

18. Ideas that do not fit into the general pattern of business. The suggestor may have a good idea but it does not apply to the particular type of work carried out by the firm.

19. Ideas badly presented and hardly intelligible, making the suggestion impossible to evaluate. The suggestor should be interviewed by the administrator or suggestion supervisor and asked to clarify his idea, and, if it shows any promise, then he should be helped to present it in clear and concise English.

The above list is by no means complete, but it does give a broad indication of policy governing the administration of most industrial and commercial establishments. As previously stated, different firms adopt different attitudes towards acceptability of employees' suggestions and what applies to one company does not necessarily apply to another.

Eligibility of employees

There appears to be no clear-cut policy regarding employee eligibility – the rules governing suggestion schemes vary widely from company to company. In some firms, such as ICI and Pilkingtons only weekly and hourly-paid employees can take part in the scheme while other concerns which employ large numbers of manual workers, such as Perkins Engines, allow members of staff who are eligible for overtime to put forward suggestions and qualify for cash awards. Courtaulds encourages all employees who are not salaried members of the staff to submit ideas for improvement. In Fords, either hourly paid or salaried employees (up to salary grade 8) can join the scheme. At Vauxhall Motors the same conditions apply as in General Motors, ie all hourly-rate workers other than skilled men are eligible; skilled trades employees, such as tool or diemakers, electricians, etc, are expected to submit suggestions about jobs outside their immediate job assignments. Salaried employees at Vauxhall are able to receive awards for suggestions unless the nature of their work includes a responsibility to develop new ideas; and supervisory staff are usually excluded from the payroll scheme but can take advantage of a special suggestion programme (Management Cost Study) which awards goods and services instead of cash for ideas which are adopted.

In most clerical and administrative operations, including banks, building societies, and insurance companies, all staff members, except officers, managers and assistant managers, are eligible for cash awards regardless of their position, unless the suggestion concerns a specifically assigned project. In some businesses, supervisors are eligible for cash awards if the idea is beyond the scope of their job responsibility. Generally speaking, employers in commercial establishments adopt a fairly liberal attitude towards eligibility of employees and the only qualification is that 'suggestions should go beyond what is expected of the suggestors in the course of their normal duties'. The Civil Service places no restrictions on staff putting forward ideas for improvement and the Model Staff Suggestion Scheme prepared for the guidance of Government Departments states: 'No officer is debarred by reason of grade from submitting suggestions or receiving the appropriate awards, though naturally the more senior the officer the more significant it becomes for the Committee to be satisfied that the suggestion is outside the scope of his normal duties'.

The Shell UK Administrative Services Suggestion Scheme is only one of ten within the Shell UK Group and was formed in 1979. To date, the company has received approximately 300 ideas, 25% of which have been viable and cost effective. The Shell scheme is open to all members of staff in Shell Centre and the Shell-Mex House buildings but only non-managerial staff are eligible for monetary awards. Awards are not made for certain types of ideas, eg those relating to pay and conditions of employment. Awards for health and safety are made at the discretion of the manager of Shell UK Administrative Services and are likely to be non-monetary.

In the United States the Government Awards Program is open to all employees and applies to members of the armed forces and all federal agencies and departments.

It is interesting to note that an increasing number of companies, both industrial and commercial, are relaxing their rules regarding eligibility of employees, although the tendency still is to exclude management staff from cash awards. IBM in the United Kingdom allows all employees, permanent, temporary and retired, to submit suggestions with the exception of members of management with the title of manager and above and people actually working in the Suggestions Department. Kodak follow more or less the same ruling.

Flexibility in interpreting eligibility

If a company adopts too rigid an attitude regarding a worker's immediate job assignment/responsibilities and excludes him from taking part in the suggestion scheme, it runs the risk of losing his goodwill and perhaps missing a number of valuable ideas for improvement. The view taken by some firms is that no exception can be made, as once the door is open to other employees in the same category the impression is given that other rules governing the scheme can be ignored. The philosophy of Philips Petroleum, however, is to favour employees when suggestions fall in the grey area. When drawing up the rules governing the scheme great care needs to be taken to see that they are simple to understand and follow. One of the best examples of clarity is afforded by ICI: 'Any employee may offer suggestions and the only suggestions which are not eligible for an award are those which an employee should be expected to make as part of his/her job including ideas which he/she could put into effect without seeking authority to do so'.

Thus eligibility can be determined by asking the employee two simple questions:

1. Could you put your idea into practice without asking your immediate superior for permission? If the answer is NO then the suggestion is eligible for an award.
2. If you had put forward the suggestion would you in fact be doing your job properly? If the answer is YES, then the suggestion is not eligible for an award.

Some of the confusion and general frustration which arises from badly-framed rules can be avoided if the terms of reference of each job are known and understood. Too often there is a great deal of vagueness about the employee's actual job responsibility or what constitutes his normal duties in terms of responsibility for develop-ment in the particular area related to a suggestion. It is realised, of course, that in a very large organisation where a wide range of subjects is covered by suggestions, it is difficult to give precise guidance to cover all definitions of normal duties. Problems can sometimes arise with staff where the suggestion has been the result of a direction from a superior requesting application of special knowledge, training, or experience to a problem, or where the suggestor is associated with the working of a group or committee responsible for studying and reporting on new plant or new methods.

When considering eligibility a great deal depends on the real purpose of the suggestion scheme. If it is mainly designed as part of an industrial participation package to improve job attitudes and create a better work environment then it makes good sense to restrict the scheme to weekly or hourly-paid workers but, if it has a genuine commercial purpose to encourage money-saving ideas, then every effort should be made to widen the scope by bringing in salaried staff and technical grades.

While the importance of simple modifications involving minor plant changes should not be underrated, what industry badly needs is more ideas of high calibre that will improve efficiency and cut the costs of the main process operations; the only way to make this possible is to encourage employees with more specialised knowledge and experience to join the scheme.

4. Awards

Tangible savings

An award serves two vitally important purposes, it rewards suggestors for worthwhile ideas and encourages further support for the scheme. While it is not possible to say what constitutes a suitable award, this being determined by the usefulness of the idea to the firm, there is little doubt that generous awards attract more suggestions of substance and stimulate greater and more lasting interest than poor awards. A multiplicity of small awards encourages a multiplicity of trivial ideas which are of little value and clog up the administrative machinery.

Many of the larger and more successful firms have no specified limit for their awards, these being based on an agreed percentage of, for example, the first year's net savings. This is easily the simplest and most equitable method of working and avoids any criticism from the shop floor that the management is securing profitable ideas at bargain prices. It is essential that the fullest publicity should be given to the award scale and the firm's method of calculating awards so that no misunderstanding arises when suggestions are adopted.

While some firms place no limit on the amount that can be paid for a suggestion, many limit it to a specific figure, eg the Ford Motor Company will not pay more than £1,000 in cash plus a new car (Escort) for any one suggestion; WD&HO Wills' awards are based on 25% of the first year's savings up to a maximum of £5,000 and Vauxhall Motors has a limit of £3,000 which, taking into account that it is tax-free compares very favourably with General Motors' top award of $10,000.

Although Britain lags behind America when it comes to major awards (eg Eastman Kodak's $47,800 for a single suggestion and IBM's $75,000), it has to be remembered that while all British awards are tax-free both American and German prize monies are subject to taxes in the region of 40%. This levelling down by the taxman makes the average American award not greatly in excess of its British equivalent.

How awards are calculated

From the company angle the most important suggestions are those which, when implemented, result in a cash saving. In the majority of cases this is comparatively easy to calculate fairly accurately, although sometimes where the evaluation has to be carried out over a period of a year or more the savings may have to be estimated.

As mentioned already the standard method adopted by most companies is to base the award on a percentage of the first year's net savings, although some firms also bring in an additional award payable on the same basis for the second consecutive year of use. The percentage varies from 10%, which is now considered to be on the low side, to as much as 50% of the net savings over the first year. According to an NASS survey of over 10,000 firms in the USA, the percentage awarded ranges from 10% to 31.7% of the first year's savings, the average being in the region of 16.6%.

Examples from British organisations

The award formula adopted by ICI varies from 10% of gross savings to 50% of net first-year savings. The net savings are obtained by spreading capital costs over five years, and the cost of tools and equipment over three years. Esso Petroleum has rather a novel method of calculating awards based on a recurring or non-recurring basis: the first £5,000 savings is at 10%, next £10,000 at 5%, £15,000 at 2.5% and all recurring savings over £30,000 at 1½%. In 1979 Esso paid out £6,166 to two Fawley Refinery workers for an idea they put forward for increasing the yield of lube feedstock.

At Vauxhall Motors suggestions which result in measurable savings in labour and/or material, productive and non-productive, are known as Class A suggestions. These qualify for the highest awards calculated at one fifth of the savings for each piece of material, multiplied by the scheduled production or usage of the piece for twelve months, divided by five. Labour savings are arrived at on the basis of the time saved on the piece multiplied by the labour cost (or rate) for the job or jobs affected by the suggestion and divided by five.

In the pharmaceutical industry, Boots gives a cash award amounting to about 10% of the first-year savings. For a suggestion which yields annual savings, cash awards of 20% of the first-year savings are made. Both the above are subject to a proportion of any capital or revenue expense incurred being subtracted from the savings before awards are calculated. The proportion of the capital element subtracted may vary from year to year; for 1986 the current figure is 25.5% this figure being calculated by the company's investment review department. Encouragement awards (usually vouchers to the value of £25) are made at the discretion of the company. No cash award is less than the value of the encouragement award. If an award exceeds £5,000 for a single suggestion the excess is counted as earnings and taxed accordingly. Suggestions where savings are incalculable, eg safety and product security, have estimated awards using a predetermined matrix, designed to reflect the financial benefit. Thereafter, the procedure for calculating an award is the same as for a suggestion with cost savings. Cost-saving ideas may be eligible for an additional award if the suggestion is implemented in other Boots factories. This additional award is calculated from 50% of the proposed net savings (ie the suggestor receives half the normal award).

Banks, building societies and to a lesser extent insurance companies in this country take an active interest in suggestion schemes for their employees and aim to generate a constant flow of ideas to benefit their company and the individuals in their day-to-day routine. Generally speaking, awards are based on a percentage of the savings that accrue from implementing suggestions and can vary from 1% to 10% of first-year savings. There is usually no minimum or maximum limit to the award paid, but in practice the highest awards very seldom exceed more than a couple of thousand pounds, although Lloyds Bank did pay out £3,685 to one member of their staff for an exceptionally brilliant idea.

Where there are current annual benefits derived from a suggestion with the Prudential Corporation the payment is based on 10% of the calculated annual benefit. This company pays a minimum award of £100 and a maximum of £1,500. No award is made for benefits of less than £1,000 per annum. With the Prudential, 50% of the award is paid upon acceptance of the suggestion and the balance upon confirmation of the first annual benefit achieved. For one-off benefits the company pays awards based on 2½% of the calculated benefit. The Minimum award is £25 and the Maximum £1,500. No award is made for benefits amounting to less than £1,000. Full payment is made upon implementation of the suggestion. For unquantifiable benefits a management panel assesses all awards, and full payment is made on implementation of the suggestion.

Suggestion schemes throughout the civil service are more generous with their award structure than most commercial firms. No limit is placed on the amount that can be paid to civil servants but recommendations for awards exceeding £10,000 have to be submitted by local suggestion committees to the central staff committee before final approval for payment is given.

Surprisingly the Inland Revenue has a well-patronised suggestion scheme for its countrywide staff of 68,000. All members of staff can take part. Identifiable continuing savings qualify for awards of 10% of first year savings of up to £22,500. Awards for suggestions above this level are based on a Cabinet office formula. There are also encouragement awards up to £25 for those ideas which are not adopted but which show constructive thought, effort or good presentation. The largest published award was for £9,000 in 1987 for a suggestion to achieve same-day banking for cheques over £10 million received in accounts offices.

In general the awards with biggest savings are those where there is a saving of a large volume of forms, accommodation, administrative costs or postage. Although a large number of suggestions are made, 4,000–5,000 a year, 95% are cleared in under a year. Up to the end of September 1987 over 4,000 suggestions had been received. Of these 703 received awards, 663 got a cash payment and about 400 suggestions were accepted. To date, £54,285 has been paid in awards. Savings resulting from these suggestions amount to £2.1 million.

Normally the full amount of savings obtained by implementing a suggestion cannot be accurately assessed until after a year. A worker in the engineering department of ICI's Bexford plant, for example, received a cheque for £2,150 in 1980 for a suggestion he made in 1978 for modifications to casting spreader units to reduce machine cleaning time and scrap. However, many companies estimate the costs and savings and pay the suggestor an interim award as soon as it has been confirmed that the estimated saving is reasonably accurate.

Examples from American companies

In some American companies, eg Cummins Engineering, the award is calculated as follows:

Material savings are determined on the basis of the value of the savings for the item, multiplied by the scheduled production or usage of it for twelve months minus 25% of any adoption costs, 15% of this amount constitutes the award. *Labour savings* are estimated on the basis of the time studied, time saved on each piece, multiplied by the estimated schedule production or usage of the piece for twelve months, multiplied by the average hourly base rate for the operation minus 25% of any adoption costs; 15% of this amount constitutes the award. Where there are both material and labour savings, the amounts are added together prior to the deduction of 25% of any adoption costs and 15% of this amount constitutes the award.

Under the Philips Petroleum Suggestion Plan the award for tangible suggestions is based on 10% of the first year's net savings. Installation costs are amortised over three years and deducted from the gross savings to determine the net savings. When measurable savings are non-recurring the full installation cost is deducted from the gross savings and the award is based on 5% of the net savings.

At Boeing the award varies according to the net savings:

Net savings	Award
$0–50	Certificate of Appreciation
$51–165	$20
$166–5000	12%
$5001–9000	$600 plus 10% of amount over 5000
$9001–62,334	$1000 plus 7.5% of amount over 9000
$62,335 and up	$5000

If a suggestion falls in the error-correction category, the maximum award is $250.

In the clerical and administrative field most British firms make much lower awards than in the manufacturing industries, but in the United States the two scales are more or less on a par. The Connecticut General Life Insurance Company pays a top award of $25,000 and a minimum of $25, awards being based on 25% of the first year's net savings. At the Chase Manhattan Bank awards range from a minimum of $25 to a maximum of $10,000 and are determined as follows:

If the suggestion results in net savings in material costs, the award will be 25% of the first year's estimated savings. If the estimated saving is in time, the suggestor receives 25% of the value of the time saved provided that the time saved is over half an hour per day per person affected. If the saving is less than half an hour, but more than ten minutes per day per person, and it can be proved that the time saved will be actually utilised, the award will be 10% of the annual estimated savings. Where there are no measurable or estimated savings from an adopted suggestion, or the time saved is ten minutes or less, then the suggestor receives an award of $25 to $100.

At Citibank a suggestion that generates savings or increases revenue for the bank qualifies for an award based on 20% of the net value of the first year's savings up to $250,000 plus 5% of the amount over $250,000. The minimum award is $25 and there is no limit to the top award. In addition there are Special Merit Awards of $100, Suggeston of the Year Awards up to $500, and Milestone Awards up to $1,000.

Each federal department and agency in the executive branch of the US government operates a suggestion programme for its employees and in 1979 $388,190 was paid out in awards to employees. The measurable benefits from suggestions amounted to $147,721,814.

Example from a European company

The Volvo Company has worked out a comprehensive system for calculating awards which is shown in Figure 2.

Figure 2: The Volvo Company system of calculating awards

The Volvo Company in Sweden has worked out a very comprehensive and all embracing system for calculating awards for employee suggestions. The information given here is kindly supplied by Volvo.

Award Standards
PROPOSALS THAT CAN BE CALCULATED
Calculation of awards:
> The basis used for the calculation of the award is primarily the net saving during the first year resulting from the suggestion. This net saving is then adjusted with respect to a number of factors which must be taken into account.
>
> They are calculated according to the following formula:

$$E = \frac{P_A}{100}\left(a \times v \times f + a \times m - \frac{k}{t}\right)\frac{P_B}{100} \times \frac{P_C}{100} \times \frac{P_D}{100}$$

E = award
P_A = adjusting factor for application conditions

P_B = adjusting factor for new feature value
P_C = adjusting factor for efforts involved in suggestion
P_D = adjusting factor for right to claim award
v = time-saving in hours per unit
a = number of units per year according to programme
f = money factors + wage fringe benefits
m = material cost decrease per unit
k = cost of application of suggested measure
t = number of years for depreciation

Utilisation period	Depreciation
1 year	1 year
1–2 years	1.5 years
2–3 years	2.5 years
3–5 years	4.0 years

Application conditions (P_a)
Award percentage related to sum of net saving during initial year

P_A – factor	Annual saving (S Kr)	Percentage
1	1 – 500	75
2	501 – 2,000	70
3	2,001 – 20,000	65
4	20,001 – 50,000	55
5	50,001 – 100,000	45
6	100,001 –	35

The above table is based on the average annual saving (approx S Kr 25,000) which can give about 55% in this factor.

New feature value (P_B)
This factor P_B is to be used when appraising the new feature value of the suggestion.

Appraisal scale – new feature value

Degree	New feature value	Percentage
1	Limited new feature value	80
2	Normal suggestion	100
3	Large new feature value	125

Efforts involved in suggestion (P_C)
To realise an idea, certain instructions and proposals are needed concerning the application of the suggestion. The efforts made in

this respect by the person submitting the suggestion can vary considerably. In some cases little effort is involved as the suggestion represents no more than an impulsive idea which is passed on to the Company through the suggestion form. The effort put into solving the problem is negligible.

In other cases the effort can be very considerable; the suggestion is well thought out and includes a constructive solution. Enclosed drawings and sketches make it possible for the suggestion to be applied according to the instructions of the person submitting it.

Appraisal scale – proposed solution

Degree	Form taken	Percentage
1	Impulse	60
2	Limited efforts	80
3	Well thought out suggestion	100
4	Comprehensive suggestion	120

Right to Award (P_D)

The association of the suggestion to the range of work of the person submitting it

This factor P_D determines the extent to which the person submitting the suggestion is entitled to an award. The decision here is made by appraising the relationship of the suggestion to the range of work, appointment or special duties carried out by the person submitting it.

Appraisal scale for right of award

Degree	Right	Percentage
1	The suggestion is completely distinct from the work carried out by the person submitting it	100
2	The suggestion concerns the work carried out by the person submitting it to a certain extent	75
3	The suggestion is associated with the work of the person submitting it and falls outside the range of such work in equal parts	50
4	The suggestion is mostly located within the field of work of the person submitting it	25
5	The suggestion is completely within the field of work of the person submitting it	0

SUGGESTIONS THAT CANNOT BE CALCULATED

In the case of suggestions concerning protective or welfare measures, a higher level of comfort or other measures for which savings cannot be calculated according to the above formula, awards are made as follows:

First of all the basic amount of the award is determined with the help of the points table for approving the utilisation of the suggestion. Then this amount is adjusted with respect to the appraisals of the suggestion from the viewpoint of new feature value, efforts involved and right to award according to P_B, P_C and P_D.

Calculation formula

E = total number of points according to table

$$\times\ 60\ SKr \times \frac{P_B}{100} \times \frac{P_C}{100} \times \frac{P_D}{100}$$

E = award

P_B = evaluation factor for new feature value of suggestion

P_C = evaluation factor for new efforts involved in suggestion

P_D = evaluation factor for new right to award

Points table

Significance of suggestion in	Degree	Small 1	Average 2	Large 3	Very large 4
Rationalisation	A	3	6	9	x
Employee protection	B	3	7	11	x
Product quality	C	3	6	9	x
High level of comfort	D	2	5	8	x
Miscellaneous	E	2	5	8	x

Note: Each point corresponds at the moment to SKr 60

EQUALISATION

The size of the award is to be equalised in such a way that the last digit is 0 or 5 per person submitting a proposal.

Intangible savings

Often there is no clear line of demarcation between a suggestion resulting in an intangible benefit and one with a tangible benefit, and it becomes largely a matter of interpretation by different managements in different types of business. It has already been pointed out that whilst some firms attach great importance to safety, eg chemical and oil companies, many concerns maintain that safety suggestions can only qualify for awards if they go beyond what can reasonably be classed as normal company practice and do not merely re-emphasise mandatory regulations.

Generally speaking, intangible suggestions are regarded more favourably by commercial than industrial organisations. Insurance companies, banks building societies and other concerns in direct touch with the public attach considerable importance to ideas for improving the quality of service and building up better customer relations. For example, Thomas Cook Ltd, the travel agent with 7,921 employees worldwide, has for several years run a very successful scheme where most of the ideas put forward by staff have been for improving customer service and are very difficult to quantify. Nevertheless, in 1986 they estimated savings amounting to £7,000 and paid out awards to the value of £2,240.

The scale of awards for intangible suggestions compares unfavourably with the scale adopted by most companies for tangible suggestions. One well-known American company, which gives a top award of $5,000 for ideas that directly improve productivity and cut costs, limits awards for intangible suggestions on safety and improved reliability to a maximum of $1,000.

The AA is one of several organisations that realise the true value of intangible suggestions where there is no possibility of actual saving. The level of awards, based on the impact of the suggestion, varies from £20 to £1,000. Although the AA suggestion scheme is to improve efficiency and working methods – so indirectly it improves the organisation's service to members – in actual practice very few suggestions directly or demonstrably impact on member service.

Three standard evaluation procedures are used to assess intangible savings.

The points system

The points system would appear to be the one best designed to give the suggestor the fairest deal as, by breaking the suggestion down into its constituent parts, it shows up its advantages as well as its disadvantages. Although every company has its own method of calculating the points gained by any one idea, the procedures followed by ICI and Vauxhall are of special interest on account of the degree of thoroughness achieved by the assessor (See Figures 3 and 4).

A number of commercial businesses, such as building societies and banks favour the point system as it reflects how far the suggestor's job covers the idea; for example, the likely extent of improvements in efficiency or service that would be gained, the scope for applying the idea within the company and the amount of work still needed to put the idea into practice.

In Woolwich Equitable Building Society's award calculation, £1 per point is given subject to a minimum of £10 (See figure 5).

Although the majority of intangible suggestions qualify for only nominal awards in the region of £25 to £30, it is possible for workers to earn much larger sums for ideas of outstanding merit. For example, at Vauxhall the maximum award for an intangible suggestion is £3,000, but it is pointed out by the Company that to qualify for such an award an idea would need to be quite outstanding and deemed to be of great importance to the Company's future.

Judgment

In some companies the suggestion committee decides on the amount of the award for an intangible suggestion on the basis of an assessment of its value by experts in a specific field, eg, the safety officer, the medical officer, or the canteen manager. While this method would appear to be acceptable in so far as the various authorities consulted are well qualified to give an expert opinion about the usefulness and applicability of the suggestions, a great deal depends on their general attitude towards the whole concept of a suggestion plan. If they resent the fact that employees are being encouraged to criticise by putting forward ideas for improvement which touch upon their areas of responsibility, then they are likely to be biased in any decisions they reach. To overcome this obstacle the administrator of the suggestion committee has to reassure the experts that the suggestions are not intended as criticisms but are aimed at improving the service.

Flat rate of assessment

Although this is by far the easiest method of evaluating intangible suggestions, it can give employees the impression that ideas in this field are not all treated seriously by management. Where suggestions relate directly to environmental conditions, such as safety and amenities, which are known directly to affect worker morale, it is important that every effort should be made to assure employees that the management is anxious to remedy any defects in working conditions and to consider all suggestions for improvements.

Figure 3: The Point System adopted by ICI for assessing all suggestions where the benefits to the company are not calculable in cash terms

Criteria
(Score no more than once from each of the following sections)

	Points
1. **Degree of adoption**	
Adopted as suggested	3
Adopted with some modification	2
Promotes valuable change which is largely or wholly different from original suggestion	1
2. **Innovation**	
Is this:	
an original idea of high innovation	3
an original idea of simple innovation	2
a new application of a little known idea	2
a new application of a well known idea	1
3. **Problem solving, identification and action**	
Has the idea promoted:	
substantial action in an area of major concern	3
action of significance in an area of concern	2
action of ordinary significance	1
4. **Extent of application**	
Significantly apply in a wide context	3
Significantly affect other jobs in plant/section	2
Apply to own job or individual situation only	1

The awards
Payment of awards will be based on the following scale:

Points	5	6	7	8	9
Awards	£35	£55	£75	£95	£120

(As at 1 June 1986)

Figure 4: Vauxhall Motors intangible suggestion award guide

This guide is intended as an aid in evaluating suggestions with intangible benefits unless they are of an outstanding or exceptional nature.

Considerations	*Evaluations*	*Point Values*

How effectively does this suggestion correct the situation?

Minor – small improvement
Moderate – goes about half way
Major – eliminates the condition
or nearly so

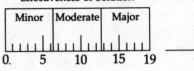

Effectiveness of Solution

How undesirable is the condition the suggestion seeks to improve?

Minor – not serious at all
Moderate – serious
Major – very serious and thus an important consideration

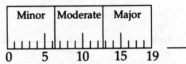

Seriousness of Condition

What are the chances of the condition occurring?

Minor – unlikely
Moderate – definite possibility
Major – definite probability

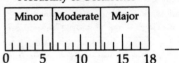

Probability of Occurrence

What portion of the employee group or what portion of operations is affected?

Minor – localised effect
Moderate – several people or several operations
Major – affects many people or operations

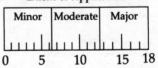

Extent of Application

How valuable is the suggestion as indicated by the cost to adopt or install it?

Minor – less than £50
Moderate – between £50–£150
Major – over £150

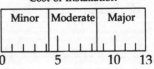

Cost of Installation

How much initiative, imagination
or ingenuity is shown?

Minor – used elsewhere in plant,
an old idea reinstated, little
original thinking

Moderate – average originality or
application

Major – clever, unique or original

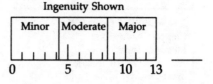

Total Points: _____ at £50 = _____

Consideration of other benefits: estimated savings _____

actual savings _____

total savings _____ × 1/5 = _____

TOTAL AWARD _____
(*Maximum award £3,000*)

A guide which can be helpful in evaluating Class 'C' suggestions for awards is:

Degree of benefit or improvement	*Points*
Major	50
Substantial	40
Moderate	25
Minor	10

Originality	*Factor*
Idea not known to be used elsewhere	6
Idea used by other industry	4
Idea already in use elsewhere in the divison	2

Application	*Factor*
General – used throughout plant or division	5
Local – more than one application in one or more departments	3
Restricted – used in one application only	1

Calculation is then made as follows:

Point Value × Originality Factor × Application Factor = Award.

Figure 5: Woolwich Equitable Building Society – use of the points system

---

1. **Responsibility factor (R)**
Completely outside	4
Mostly outside	3
Part inside – part outside	2
Mostly inside	1
Completely inside	0
Maximum score R = 4)	

---

2. **Improvement Factor (I)**. Each element scores:

Product competitiveness	3	2	1	0
Quality of service	3	2	1	0
Public relations	3	2	1	0
Employee relations	3	2	1	0
Administrative procedures	3	2	1	0
Working conditions	3	2	1	0
Job satisfaction	3	2	1	0
(Maximum score 1 = 21)				

---

3. **Number Factor (N)**
All customers and/or staff	4
All branch. HQ staff	3
Own region/area/departmental staff	2
Own branch/section staff	1
(Maximum score N = 4)	

---

4. **Adoption factor (A)**
No further work required	5
Some research and modification	3
Development of a new idea	1
(prompted by original suggestion)	
(Maximum score A = 5)	

Award = $R \times I \times N \times A$
(Maximum points = $4 \times 21 \times 4 \times 5 = 1,680$)

Complaints arising from low awards

While it is relatively easy to compute the savings brought about by substituting a shorter bolt for a longer one or using an unplated fastener instead of a chrome-plated one in a car assembly, there is no reliable yardstick for measuring the true value of a suggestion to improve product quality or safety practices which reduce hazards.

The easy way out of this difficulty is to make arbitrary awards which bear little relation to the true value of these suggestions.

Ideas put forward for improving safety practices are often grossly undervalued and this in spite of abundant proof that accidents can cost a company a great deal of money. A few years ago the Dow Chemical Company produced a report which showed that the average disability accident can cost 1,400 hours in lost production time, lost time to supervision, accident committee costs, committee time, safety training, design and revision committees, transportation, medical and therapy costs, and discussions on safety. In short, intangible suggestions can produce tangible results.

There needs to be some re-thinking about awards for intangible suggestions to bring them more in line with those for tangible ideas. In some branches of the motor industry it is significant that increasing attention is being given to quality control because it is now realised that it has a very positive effect on marketing and averting vehicle recall. Although the points system for assessing awards goes some way towards arriving at a just and equitable standard of payment, there is still need for more generous treatment so as to encourage employees to give more attention to such important matters as improvements in working conditions, better morale and elimination of hazards; all of which make possible increased efficiency.

A suggestion scheme with no awards

While awards are usually regarded as providing the necessary incentives to make employee suggestion schemes work, Texas Instruments in Bedford, has formed a scheme with a different objective: to keep people happy. It is aptly called 'Speak Up' and draws the attention of management to employees' suggestions, complaints and comments about working conditions and the environment. The scheme manages to get positive results within five working days. Instead of bottling up their feelings, the Texas staff just 'Speak Up'.

The personnel officer, Susan Lapthorne, manages the scheme with the help of the latest electronic devices. If an employee has a suggestion to make, he or she writes it down on one of the 'Speak Up' forms readily available throughout the site and sends it to her via the Texas electronic mail system. She acknowledges receipt of the suggestion and passes it on to the appropriate manager for a full answer. The manager should reply within five working days of the acknowledgement with a copy to the co-ordinator. Susan

Lapthorne logs all replies on a Lotus spread sheet and analyses the type of inputs received. She also logs the type of responses managers are giving, ie explanations, positive responses.

All this information is fed to the 'Speak Up' committee and then to the Issues and Corrective Action Team. The greatest care is taken throughout the exercise to ensure prompt action and employees can always rely upon their suggestions being considered sympathetically.

Texas Instruments does not offer any rewards for suggestions via the 'Speak Up' scheme. Reports of the 'Speak Up' scheme are frequently published in the Texas newspaper *Tidings*. In the United States a number of companies have similar non-award schemes which they find very popular.

Miscellaneous awards

Modification awards

Where a suggestion holds the germ of a useful idea but, in its present form, cannot be adopted without modification, a number of companies give a modification award (sometimes known as *Near Misses*). This is left to the discretion of the management but it is usually based on an assessment of the value of the original idea. Eastman Kodak gives an award in all those cases where the suggestion requires modification before it can be adopted and bases payment on the value of the modification. Where independent action is taken after a suggestion has been investigated, but no adopted, and held in retention, an award is payable if the conditions for re-investigation are met.

Awards of £50–£100 are often given for suggestions showing great promise but requiring further research and development before they can be adopted.

Supplementary awards

These are sometimes made for suggestions which, on review, prove to be more valuable than they appeared to be when first considered. A few big companies review at six-monthly intervals all those suggestions which may be likely to qualify for a supplementary award.

Acceptance and recognition awards

A few companies give an initial small award for each eligible suggestion accepted by the suggestion committee for consideration. The Bell Telephone Company gives an initial award of $25 for each suggestion accepted by the approval committee in addition to any further award that may be granted later.

Consolation/encouragement awards

These are given for suggestions which show ingenuity, interest and originality but cannot be implemented for various reasons. For example, a fitter in an engineering works making parts for washing machines suggested that one particularly difficult welding operation could be done more efficiently by using a robot. Management felt, however, that although the idea was sound, the high capital expenditure could not be justified and before robots could be introduced their installation had to be agreed with the unions.

One of the main purposes of the award is to encourage first-time suggestors whose ideas have been rejected. The danger is that it tends to encourage a mass of trivial suggestions which cause delays in processing worthwhile ideas and create problems as regards consistency of treatment.

Occasionally an award is made where a suggestor defines a problem but fails to provide an answer. Normally this type of suggestion is rejected, but it can happen that the problem itself may be an important one which has escaped the attention of management. The Chloride Group of Companies calls this particular award a *Highlight Award* and finds that it serves a useful purpose by encouraging employees to keep the lower echelons of management fully in the picture regarding shop floor problems affecting material handling, safety, health hazards and quality control.

Some firms refer to these awards as *Thoughtful Awards*, for example the Abbey National Building Society includes this type of award in its rule book and gives £50 for ideas which show evidence of creative thought, innovation, research and presentation.

Special merit awards

A number of American companies review all accepted suggestions every six months and those considered to be of outstanding merit are given additional awards ranging from $50 to $1,000.

Wake-up awards

So-called 'wake-up' awards are occasionally given for all adopted suggestions that do not result in any tangible saving. The Cummins Engine Company in the United States believes that this award acts as an encouragement to potential suggestors. No set figure is given for the award, the amount being determined by the awards committee.

Impetus awards

This type of award is sometimes given for an accepted suggestion which does not present a new idea in itself, but merely speeds up action on a project or previous suggestion already submitted. (Since the United Airlines case in California in 1976 this type of award is now seldom given – see page 117.)

Non-monetary awards

While a cash payment is the usual type of award, a few companies also give special prizes, sometimes in addition to a cash award but more often in place of money. Ford provides a fully equipped Escort car with all £1,000 awards; Cossor gives a Suggestion of The Year Award which is a week's holiday for two valued at £250; and government departments give a wide range of goods for merit awards. Philips is one of several companies that provide small gifts to those who have consistently put forward award-winning ideas over a period of years. Suggestors who have received more than Fl.1,000 in awards over five years are given a silver tie-pin, while those who have received more than Fl.3,000 are awarded a gold tie-pin. A jewelled tie-pin is given to those in receipt of Fl.5,000 over five years. Female employees are awarded chains with pendants instead of tie-pins. The Boeing Company is one of a number of American organisations giving non-monetary awards to employees submitting suggestions of merit. These vary from coffee and doughnuts served in the shop to annual free travel in a chartered 747, pen and pencil sets, clock radios, tape recorders and similar goods. For several years Boeing has allocated to specific departments with a high suggestion record a definite quantity of $2,000 prepaid trips to a destination of the employee's choice (a favourite location being Hawaii). One of the most popular small gifts made available to successful suggestors is the Boeing golfing cap.

Temporary condition award guide

In certain industries, notably the motor industry, at the start-up of new production runs employees are encouraged to put forward suggestions for ironing out some of the inevitable teething troubles that occur in the early days of production. A guide provided by Vauxhall Motors is shown in Figure 6.

Figure 6: Vauxhall Motors start-up suggestions award guide

This guide is to be used only in evaluating those suggestions adopted at start-up of production which correct an abnormal condition. General Motors Suggestion Plan policy is to pay one-fifth of the first year's savings when savings can be measured. But, when the Suggestion Committee considers the condition to be abnormal, that it would not have been permitted to continue for a full year at the early cost rate, then this guide may be applied.

The award amount equals the percentage of the projected annual savings as shown for the appropriate length of time the operation was run before the improvement was suggested.

Length of time the operation was run before improvement was suggested	Percentage of yearly savings to be paid as award
Less than one week	2.5
One week	3.0
Two weeks	3.5
Three weeks	4.0
Four weeks	5.0
Five weeks	6.0
Six weeks	7.0
Seven weeks	8.0
Eight weeks	9.5
Nine weeks	11.5
Ten weeks	13.5
Eleven weeks	15.5
Twelve weeks	20.0

5. Administration

Setting up a suggestion scheme

The first and probably the most important step to take before actually launching a suggestion scheme is to find out what the workforce thinks of the idea. This is best achieved by carrying out an attitude survey. If carefully planned, the exercise can provide a reliable feedback of opinions untainted by management prejudices. An attitude survey also helps to build up good personal relations with the workers who may eventually be persuaded to take an active part in running the scheme.

There is no ready-made formula for designing a questionnaire to be used by the interviewers, but the professionals generally recommend focusing on four main types of question:

- An introductory question requiring a simple and straightforward answer;
- A 'what-do-you-think' question dealing with the respondent's opinions;
- A 'why-do-you-think' question; and
- 'Probe questions' which put the responsibility on the respondent for suggesting alternative ways of running a scheme.

Typical questions that might produce a useful response are:

1. Have you ever heard of a suggestion scheme?
2. Some firms run these schemes and award prizes for ideas which increase productivity, product quality and reduce waste. What do you think of the idea?
3. If this company were to set up such a scheme, would you come forward with any of your own ideas for improvements? If not, why not?
4. Have you any thoughts on the best way to run a suggestion scheme? Do you, for instance, think it a good idea to reward individuals for suggestions likely to profit the firm, or would you favour a profit-sharing scheme in which everyone shares in the savings and benefits derived from workers' suggestions.
5. Do you think that the names of employees who submit suggestions should be known or kept secret?

Although an attitude survey gives a useful indication of the interest shown by the workforce, it needs to be cross-checked by face-to-face encounters with workers' representatives, shop stewards and supervisory staff to determine the degree of co-operation that might be expected, their reservations about the scheme, and their fears for its success. Discussions should be centred round three basic questions:

1. Do you think a suggestion scheme is worthwhile in terms of actual benefits to the workers and savings to the company?
2. Will the trade unions participate in running the scheme?
3. If the scheme goes forward, will charge-hands, foremen, supervisors, etc, co-operate in making it a success?

It is only by a frank exchange of views that management will be able to reach a decision on whether it would be a good idea to go ahead with a scheme, leave the matter in abeyance, or reject the whole project. No general blueprint for a suggestion scheme exists, each plan needs to be carefully tailored to meet the special needs and circumstances of the factory or office. Conditions which apply quite happily to one organisation are unsuitable for another. A scheme may have to be modified a number of times before it can satisfy all parties and stand a reasonable chance of success.

Preparing the scheme

Once the scheme has been given top management approval, then it is advisable to contact people who are running successful suggestion schemes in other companies to find out at first hand some of the problems that may arise. It is also advisable to discuss the proposed venture with the Industrial Society in London. This organisation can be of considerable help as their Information Section regularly runs courses for suggestion scheme administrators and has a library of suggestion plan material available for reference.

There is always a risk that supervisory staff may tend to regard any suggestions put forward by the workers under their control as implied criticism and a reflection on their competence. It is essential therefore to make foremen and supervisors fully aware of the attitude of management. They should understand that a high return of worthwhile suggestions from their department or section will be regarded by the bosses as a clear indication that morale amongst the workers is high, and that the conditions are favourable for greater involvement in the company's business. On the other hand, a low return of suggestions will be looked upon by management with disfavour as an indication that supervisory staff are not co-operating in making the scheme a success. A notable feature of the General Motors suggestion plan is that foremen are encouraged to do everything they can to stimulate ideas from their staff. One technique which they use is to highlight current production problems and discuss with the men possible solutions which they might think about and develop into concrete suggestions.

At an early stage in the planning, training courses should be organised for shop stewards so that they are well briefed in the aims of the scheme and how it is to operate for the mutual benefit of both workers and management.

Functions of administrators

One of the main criticisms of many schemes is that they are remote from the shop floor and out-of-touch with potential suggestors. It is essential for each works or office to have an identified, knowledgeable person responsible for running the scheme, preferably someone with shop-floor experience or a working knowledge of the operations and procedures. The closer and more personal the contact with the suggestors, the better the prospects are for the success of the scheme.

Experience tends to show that suggestion systems with full-time administrators have a far better chance of survival than those run by part-time personnel. An administrator who enjoys the confidence of both management and the workforce inspires the feeling that he will make sure the employee gets a square deal.

At the Perkins Engines works in Peterborough, which has one of the most successful schemes in Britain, the administrator has both engineering and shop-floor experience. He handles on average some 60 suggestions a week. He ensures that all suggestions are progressed in the minimum time and advises on all aspects of the scheme from the time suggestions reach the suggestion office to the moment when they are passed to the suggestion scheme committee. The manager's function is to examine all submitted suggestions for duplication and practical value, notify suggestors of acceptance or non-acceptance and, where doubt exists about an employee's idea for an improvement, to discuss the matter with him and prevent any misunderstanding. In this instance the manager has a technical background and considerable works experience, so he is well qualified to assess the value of any suggestion and to decide whether it should be processed further and eventually passed to the suggestion committee for final evaluation or assessment. Provided the administrator is well qualified and enjoys the full confidence of the workforce, as is the case at Perkins Engines, he can do a great deal to ease the pressure on the suggestion committee and so help to reduce the turn-round time for suggestions.

In some American companies where there are a number of plants each manager appoints his own suggestion administrator, who is responsible for the day-to-day working of the scheme but has no authority to reject suggestions or to recommend awards. These are matters which are dealt with by committees. At General Motors the suggestion plan supervisor is responsible for the successful operation of the scheme. Specific responsibilities include:

- Receiving suggestions;
- Acknowledging suggestions;
- Preparing investigated suggestions for review and action by the suggestion committee;
- Supervising the payment and presentation of awards;
- Notifying suggestors of the non-acceptance of their suggestions;
- Maintaining necessary suggestion files and records;
- Destroying records at the end of six years after final action;
- Promoting and publicising the plan;
- Conducting educational work with supervision;
- Preparing necessary reports; and
- Supervising suggestion plan personnel.

The supervisor also acts as chairman of the committee.

Committees

Although some organisations operate suggestion schemes quite successfully without the aid of a suggestion committee, there is throughout industry a general preference for an independent body to act as a final adjudicator. It is felt that its decisions are less likely to be challenged than those made by one or more individuals, no matter how well qualified they may be.

As a rule the suggestion committee should never be too far removed from the field of operations. Central committees often lack credibility because of their remoteness from the shop floor, infrequency of their meetings and the inevitable delays in reaching any decisions and making awards. In the United Kingdom many firms now favour plant suggestion committees. These are close to the shop floor, their members are known to the workforce, and, because they meet once a week, they are able to deal with the business promptly and make quick decisions so that the minimum delay is encountered in notifying suggestors.

Boots has several pharmaceutical factories throughout the United Kingdom and each one has a committee of four, comprising the factory manager or assistant factory manager, who takes the chair; the factory or area engineer; the suggestions scheme administrator; and the investigating expert, who may be a departmental manager. Once a suggestion has been accepted into the Boots system, evaluation of its merits becomes automatic. It is then the responsibility of the factory suggestion scheme committee to ensure that it is checked for correctness and eligibility, and, if it is accepted, registered into the scheme. Past records are examined to ensure that the suggestion has not been submitted before. Once the suggestion is passed to the chairman of the committee it is sent to a selected assessor for evaluation. When this is done the evaluated suggestion is discussed at the meeting and, if an award is to be made, the type of award and the amount is determined. The proposed savings are checked and signed by the factory accountant and details of the suggestion and the proposed award are then passed to the investment review for final approval.

When approved, a cheque is obtained from the expense account section and forwarded to the chairman of the committee for presentation to the suggestor by the factory manager or departmental head. Approved awards below £25 are paid immediately in Boots Gift Vouchers. In addition to the factory suggestions committee, Boots have a suggestions steering committee made up of six senior members of the staff with a secretary. They meet at six-monthly intervals to review the operation of the scheme throughout the company in accordance with the rules of the suggestion scheme set out in the Boots procedure manual, to rule on eligibility and to receive the annual report from the administrator, and to make recommendations for improvement.

A variety of committees are often used to carry out the different functions of schemes. Awards are made by an awards committee appointed by the plant manager; suggestion administrator committees, made up of plant administrators, look after records, review awards and deal with all administrative problems.

Sometimes a suggestion policy committee, with members drawn from senior management, is given overall responsibility for the suggestion plan.

Constitution of committees

There exists a wide difference of opinion regarding the membership of committees and while some organisations select only management representatives, others include two or more employee representatives or union men. STC's suggestion scheme, which is operated on a divisional basis, leaves selection of committee members to the division or unit manager who usually appoints a chairman, secretary, two employee representatives, a cost accountant, a methods/industrial engineer, and a personnel officer. Vauxhall Motors picks only management representatives and leaves the choice of members to the plant manager. Philips is another large company that has only management representatives on its committee. The feeling behind the general preference shown for selecting only management members is that they have the experience and knowledge of operations best fitted for evaluating employees' suggestions and, as they occupy important positions in the company they are able to speak with authority.

It has to be recognised, however, that committees made up entirely of management are often subject to criticism because of their remoteness from the suggestors, many of whom believe that the members lean too heavily on the company side when it comes to making high awards. It is vitally important that a suggestion committee should not only act fairly and squarely in making decisions but should be seen to act in this way so as to dispel all doubts about company bias.

Where employee representatives or union men are not members of the suggestion committee, it is recommended that the suggestion administrator whose day-to-day concern is the running of the scheme and who is in constant touch with employees should be chosen as chairman of the committee. This would remove any feeling that the committee was too remote from the shop floor. At Firestone the accepted practice at all participating locations is for the plant manager to appoint the members of the suggestion board and for the suggestion co-ordinator or administrator to be the non-voting chairman. Those chosen to serve on the board are the plant engineer or representative, plant controller or his representative, maintenance department manager, production manager, safety engineer, and any other members as needed.

British Telecom keeps the bureaucracy down to a minimum and restrict the number of members of their Awards and Valuation Committee to four; these consist of the Head of Business Planning/ Efficiency, the Suggestions Scheme Manager, a Financial Advisor plus one other. Expert advice is brought in as necessary.

Sub-committees for preliminary vetting

In firms where joint consultation is practised it is now customary to filter all suggestions through a sub-committee for preliminary scrutiny and evaluation before sending them on to the formal suggestion committee. At ICI this informal plant group is made up of the group manager, supervisor, shop steward and the suggestor himself. It holds two meetings, one following the other very quickly. The first is aimed at understanding and developing the idea in collaboration with the suggestor, and establishing evaluation needs and wider application. The second meeting sets out to reach agreement about adoption and points assessment for intangible suggestions, to make small awards for some ideas up to the agreed limit, and to forward its recommendations for larger awards to the suggestion committee for a final decision. One important advantage of this informal group is that it is organised on a local level and enjoys the full confidence of the workforce.

By involving the suggestor in discussions about the merits of his idea at an early stage he is given an opportunity to explain how his improvement works and what it will achieve. An informal face-to-face discussion prevents any misunderstanding which may arise from reading the description of the suggestion as set out on the suggestion form. It has to be remembered that for some employees written communications are something of an ordeal.

Evaluation of suggestions by committees

This is the most difficult task facing the committee. Evaluation calls for good judgment, a sense of fair play, intimate knowledge of the subjects under consideration, and a willingness to weigh in the balance the opinions of those departments most concerned in implementing the suggestions. The committee will also need to take note of any recommendation or opinions expressed by the suggestor's supervisor or foreman who has first-hand knowledge of the idea under consideration. Assessing the awards for adopted suggestions must always be a difficult exercise for the committee as their decisions have to be based on an agreed figure for the savings which the company would hope to make by implementing the improvement. Quite obviously at this discussion stage it is only possible to arrive at an approximate figure for the first year's net saving resulting from introducing the improvement, and an interim award is paid, but scrupulous care has to be taken to ensure that each decision does full justice to the company and the suggestor.

Functions of committees

The committee is responsible both to the management and the workforce for the administration of the suggestion scheme. The specific responsibilities of the committee can best be summarised as follows:

1. Receive suggestions and ensure that they have been registered and acknowledged.
2. Consider investigated reports on suggestions and accept or reject on the basis of the recommendations by the suggestion supervisor or administrator and the departmental experts who have been consulted.
3. Recommend payment of encouragement and other special awards where they can do the most good in promoting the scheme.
4. Determine the amount of award and authorise payment.
5. Make arrangements for the presentation of major awards to be carried out by senior management representatives and smaller awards by foreman or supervisor. Ensure that each presentation is given full publicity so as to extend well-deserved personal recognition to the employee earning the award.
6. Notify those suggestors whose ideas have been rejected and, where possible, make sure that their supervisors explain in person the reasons for their rejection.
7. Authorise re-investigation of suggestions if results of previous enquiries are inconclusive.
8. Deal with any complaints.
9. Recommend improvements to the scheme for the consideration of management.
10. Make certain that the suggestion office maintains all necessary records and handles all suggestions promptly.
11. Develop and institute promotional and publicity campaigns.
12. Review all suggestions held in the file after a two-year period has elapsed since the date when first considered by the committee and make further awards where justified. (Note: Some companies hold

suggestions for one year only, others for longer periods – up to seven years.)
13. Destroy records at the end of whatever period is decided after final action.

Methods and procedures

Anonymity

One decision that has to be made at an early stage of planning the operation and discussing administration is the identification of suggestors. Some companies like International Computers Limited maintain that they should remain anonymous until the final decision is made by the suggestion committee. Once the suggestion form has been registered and given a number, no-one except the suggestion award officer knows whose name was on the original form. This practice ensures that assessment and evaluation of the idea are fair and impartial. If no award is made, the name of the suggestor is not revealed.

A strong argument against secrecy is that it is impersonal and remote from employees. Perkins Engines believe that personal contact should be maintained at every stage so that any uncertainties or problems can be discussed with the suggestor. This view is shared by many large concerns, though some, such as Vauxhall Motors, give the suggestor the option of remaining anonymous by putting an X in the box provided on the suggestion form where it reads: 'If you would prefer no publicity, put X here'.

The suggestion form

This should be as simple and straightforward as possible with the minimum of instructions and advice printed on the front and the rules of the scheme on the back. The suggestion form used by Hotpoint Limited satisfies all these requirements (see Figure 7). Plenty of space is allocated for describing the suggestion and providing details of the machine or tool referred to in the suggestion. On the back of the form, the top section, which is detachable, has to be filled in by the suggestor and, after being registered at the suggestion office and given a number, is returned to the suggestor. This slip fulfils a dual purpose: it is an official receipt and also an acknowledgement.

The A T & T (UK) Limited suggestion form (see Figure 9), which is provided with three attached carbon copy sheets for office use, should present no difficulty to the suggestor. On the back of the form (Figure 10) the suggestion plan rules are set out very clearly and there is information about eligible employees, eligible suggestions, awards and appeal procedure.

Suggestion boxes

Strategically placed suggestion boxes offer two important advantages. First, they are accessible and, second, they lend themselves readily to forms of display drawing attention to the scheme. Boxes need to be maintained in good condition and emptied twice a week.

While it has been said that some employees do not like being seen dropping suggestion forms into the boxes, the majority much prefer this method as it is simple, preserves a reasonable degree of confidentiality and, as the boxes are placed at convenient points in the works or offices, they are easily accessible. The alternative is to use the company's internal mail for sending the forms to the suggestion office, but this is not as simple as it may first appear to be as the forms and the pre-addressed envelopes have first to be obtained from the office which may be some distance away. With suggestion boxes there are always supplies of forms made available in racks nearby so that the potential suggestor has everything available on the spot.

Office procedure

Success in operating a suggestion scheme depends to a large extent on the way in which the suggestion office is organised. The work needs to be handled quickly and efficiently so that the minimum delay is experienced in processing the suggestions. Procedures vary a good deal from company to company but the method used by the Philips Petroleum Company is of particular interest as it is simple, straightforward and yet satisfies all the requirements:

1. Suggestions are stamped in consecutive numerical order. They are then classified by type according to a coding system.
2. The files are checked to see that the suggestion is not identical to

Hotpoint

Please read notes overleaf before filling in form.

Suggestion Form

№ 61996

BOX No. 3 IF ADOPTED MY SUGGESTION WILL:	BOX No. 1 FACTORY OR DIVISION
	SUGGESTION CONCERNS DEPT.
	DATE:
*	USE BLOCK LETTERS

DETAILED DESCRIPTION OF SUGGESTION.

FOR OFFICE USE ONLY

CIRCULATION				
DATE				

THIS IS YOUR SUGGESTION IDENTIFICATION SLIP – KEEP IT TO CLAIM YOUR AWARD.

NAME	DEPARTMENT	DATE	№ 61996

OFFICE USE ONLY	RESULTS LIST FOR MONTH			
	AWARDS PAID BY CASHIER			
	DATE OF PAYMENT			

Figure 7: Form used for the Hotpoint Suggestion Scheme

Suggestion Form

FOR OFFICE USE ONLY

AWARD				
DATE				

If you have an idea, ANY IDEA, that you feel may benefit the Company in any way, fill in this form and place in the suggestion box or send in the internal mail to the Suggestions Administrator.

To enable the evaluation of your suggestion to be carried out, please fill in this form as follows:—

(1) Complete Box No. 1 with the date, the factory or division of the Company you work in and the area concerned by your idea. If you are a staff employee you must also complete Box No. 2.

(2) Complete Box No. 3 with a brief outline of what your suggestion will achieve.

(3) Now write out your suggestion with as much detail as possible. Extra sheets may be used if necessary. It is often a good idea to prepare a rough sketch of your suggestion. You don't have to be an artist, the presentation of your idea is what is really wanted Please use Part Numbers if possible when referring to piece parts (your supervisor will tell you the number if you are not sure). In many cases the actual piece part may be sent with the suggestion to help explain your idea. You may also be able to make a model of your idea that will assist in explaining its value to the Company.

Please write the suggestion number from this form on to any additional pieces of paper or drawing, etc. you wish to submit with your suggestion.

(4) When you have completed the form and given all the information you can, read it through again just to make sure you have not missed anything out. Now fill in the slip at the bottom of the form. Detach this slip from the form and keep in a safe place.

(5) Attach all sheets together and place in the Suggestion box or send in the internal mail to the Suggestions Administrator.

The progress of your suggestion will be reported on the Suggestion Bulletin published on the Suggestions Notice Board each month.

Any award made for your suggestion can be collected from the wages office on presentation of your slip at the times agreed by your local management.

NOTE. If you have any queries regarding any aspect of the Suggestion Scheme, your Suggestions Administrator will be pleased to help.

BOX No. 2 STAFF ONLY	NAME _____	POSITION _____

Hotpoint   **SUGGESTION SCHEME**

Figure 8: Reverse side of the Hotpoint Suggestion Scheme form

SUGGESTION FORM

PE-033
(06-87)

IDEAS FOR ACTION

AT&T

SUGGESTION NUMBER			
RECEIPT DATE			
SUGGESTER'S LEGAL NAME	SOCIAL SECURITY #	POSITION TITLE	SALARY GRADE
COMPLETE BUSINESS ADDRESS			PHONE #

Explain in Detail: 1) The condition, problem, material affected. 2) What should be done about it. (Attach supportive information, sketches, etc.)
3) How the company will benefit. (Give specific work-hours, materials or dollars saved, revenue increased, etc.)

If you submitted this suggestion before, what was the Assigned Number? _____

Write or type clearly. Make sure all copies are legible.

Page ____ of ____

I understand and accept the conditions that relate to my (our) submission as described on the reverse side of the form in the **Ideas for Action Rules**.

Suggester's Signature	Date

Suggester keeps *gold* copy. Send all other copies to Suggestion Program Office.

Figure 9: AT&T Suggestion form

IDEAS FOR ACTION RULES

GENERAL

Terms and conditions of this AT&T Suggestion Program are detailed in the "Ideas For Action" Policies and Procedures Manual kept on file in the Employee Suggestion Office.

In the event of any inconsistencies between the Suggestion Form and the Policies and Procedures Manual, the latter shall prevail.

All suggestions must be submitted on an official Ideas For Action Suggestion Form and signed by the suggester(s). When submitting more than one suggestion, use a separate form for each.

When more than one suggester is involved in submitting an idea, the additional suggesters' names, social security numbers, position titles, salary grades, business addresses, telephone numbers and <u>signature(s)</u> should be listed on a separate sheet of paper.

Upon submission, all suggestions become the exclusive property of AT&T. The Company retains the right to all decisions on matters relating to each suggestion.

AT&T reserves the right to modify, amend, or discontinue the Ideas for Action Suggestion Program at any time.

ELIGIBILITY

All AT&T employees are eligible to participate in the Ideas for Action Suggestion Program, but only second level managers and below in participating entities are eligible for awards.

Department Chiefs, Section Chiefs, Technical Professionals and Engineer Associates are <u>ONLY</u> eligible when suggestions are outside their scope of responsibility or do not involve a manufacturing location. They may be eligible for cash awards for entity-wide issues.

Awards cannot be paid if the subject matter of the suggestion is or was, within the last six months, part of the suggester's specifically assigned job responsibilities.

AWARDS

AT&T retains the sole, exclusive right to accept a suggestion, to decide the amount of the award, if any, and to determine when the award will be paid.

Awards for the measurable, tangible results of accepted suggestions will be based on 20% of the first year's net savings (savings and/or revenues less cost of implementing the suggestion). Awards for non-measurable accepted suggestions will be determined by AT&T based on an intangible awards scale.

The minimum award is $50. The maximum award is $20,000. All awards are subject to income tax, payable by the recipient.

If the same suggestion is submitted independently by different employees, only the suggestion first received at the Suggestion Program Office shall be eligible for an award.

TIME LIMIT

All non-accepted suggestions are award eligible for one year from the receipt date stamped on each Evaluation Form. If the idea is implemented during this one year period, it is the suggester's responsibility to bring this to the attention of the Suggestion Office so that the cost savings and award amount can be determined. If the suggestion is not implemented during this one year period and the suggester believes the idea still has merit, further award consideration will be granted if the idea is re-submitted on a new suggestion form.

INELIGIBLE SUGGESTIONS

Suggestions in the following categories will be considered ineligible for acceptance in the Ideas for Action Suggestion Program.

- Matters covered by collective bargaining.
- Unsatisfactory conditions correctible through normal procedures or supervisory action.
- Minor errors or omissions in forms, drawings, practices and other informational media.
- Pension and disability plans, salary, wages, personnel changes, employee benefits and commemorative gifts (except where changes to administrative processes apply).
- Ideas that violate legal obligations.
- Employee-patented or copyrighted items.
- Slogans or media advertising ideas.
- Procedures, materials, etc. already in use, or under study by AT&T.
- Indefinite statements or observations that "something should be done" without offering a means of achieving improvement.

BY SIGNING THIS FORM

- AT&T employees agree to be contacted by and to discuss their suggestion with an Ideas for Action Suggestion Program evaluator who may ask for additional information and/or clarifications.
- Employees agree to permit AT&T to publicize the suggestion. The suggester's name or photo may be used in this regard.
- Employees recognize it as a contract and agree to abide by the rules and guidelines of the Ideas for Action Suggestion Program.

MAIL SUGGESTIONS TO:

AT&T
Suggestion Program Office
*150 JFK Parkway, Room 3B214
Short Hills, New Jersey 07078

Interoffice = JK-3B214

Employees at factory locations should submit their suggestions, using this form, to the Suggestion Coordinator at their location.

FOR MORE INFORMATION OR ADDITIONAL FORMS CALL:
1-800-341-2263

Figure 10: Reverse side of the AT&T form

one previously submitted. If the suggestion is a duplicate, the suggestor is told immediately that his suggestion is ineligible for an award.

3. Suggestion record cards are made up in duplicate for each suggestion. A history card is also completed.

4. An acknowledgement card is sent to each suggestor whose suggestion is to be processed.

5. After the suggestion has been recorded in a pending file for follow-up purposes, it is routed to the supervisor or department head in the area affected by the suggestion.

6. The department or supervisor attaches his comments to the suggestion and returns it to the suggestion plan administrator. The administrator may accept the comments or continue pursuing the matter until sufficient information is obtained to evaluate the merit of the suggestion.

7. A file is kept on pending suggestions. If a suggestion has been pending for 30 days, the suggestor is told that it is still under investigation.

8. When the administrator feels that the comments on the suggestion are adequate, photostats of both suggestions and comments are sent to each member of the award committee.

9. The committee discusses the suggestions and approves, or requests further investigation. If a suggestion is approved, the committee determines the amount of the award.

10. If the committee does not agree with the decision handed down by a supervisor, the administrator prepares a memorandum to the department head stating the reasons for disagreement.

11. Whenever a suggestion is not approved, the employee is sent a personal letter by the administrator explaining the reasons for its rejection. If the suggestor disagrees with the decision and furnishes the administrator with further reasons for the adoption of the idea, the case may be re-opened.

12. Award cheques for all approved suggestions are paid to the suggestor promptly.

Some large companies and organisations, such as the Inland Revenue, have found that by introducing computer-based systems considerable economies can be effected in staff and the whole process of control speeded up and made much more efficient. Checking up duplicate suggestions, always a laborious and time-consuming job, can be accomplished in a matter of minutes with a computer. What is particularly satisfying about computerised systems is that tasks such as the analysis of suggestions – which previously involved a great deal of tedious work – now present few difficulties and can be done in a fraction of the time formerly employed.

Computerised databases can be manipulated, sieved and combined so as to give valuable patterns of information that enable the suggestion administration team to have a better insight into the potential of suggestors. Andrew Neil, editor of the *Sunday Times*, and John Humphrys of the BBC, have made a special study of business videos and recommend the Ashton Tate's Basel IV running on IBM PS/2 microcomputer. According to their research, this would seem to be the ideal equipment for storing information on personal records and details of ideas submitted by the workforce. A high standard of efficiency can be achieved by processing the information in the database. In its simplest form – say a list of suggestors – the database can be sieved so as to find at a glance those who produce ideas which win awards of £50 and over and those who never manage to have any of their ideas adopted.

In some companies great care is taken to involve the suggestor in all preliminary discussions about his idea so that he is given every opportunity to present his improvement in the most favourable light. Although this procedure is in many ways excellent, it is only possible in works where there are relatively few employees, such as chemical plants, oil refineries, food processing factories and the like: the ICI suggestion scheme has been developed on a person-to-person basis that stresses employee involvement through every step of the investigation and evaluation of the idea.

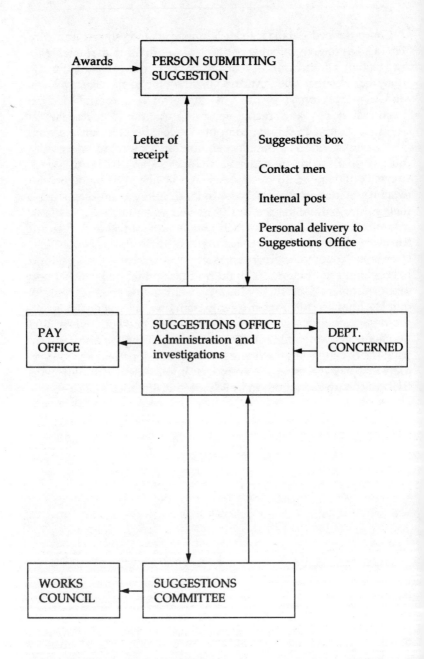

Figure 11: Suggestion handling procedures

6. Evaluations, Rejections and Reviews

Turn-round time

A long delay in reaching a decision about the usefulness of a suggestion reflects adversely on the scheme. The originators of ideas for improvement are naturally impatient to know whether their suggestions have been accepted or rejected. The key element in continued participation in a suggestion plan is the way in which the evaluation is carried out – is it thorough, scrupulously fair, and speedy? Comparatively few suggestions are highly complex and necessitate protracted testing and experimental work; the majority call for simple, straightforward evaluation which can be carried out quickly. If ideas have to be referred to several different sections of the organisation for expert opinions and long delays in reaching decisions are inevitable, then this should be explained to the suggestor. The more people who have to be consulted in reaching a decision, the longer the turn-round time. It is therefore important that every effort should be made to reduce the number of consultants so as to cut down the processing time and also to reduce the cost to the company in terms of man-hours spent on the evaluation.

Some line managers have the mistaken idea that if a suggestion is processed too quickly the suggestor is given the impression that his idea has not had the full treatment it merits, so they are not in favour of quick decisions but prefer to keep the suggestor in suspense for three or four weeks. Manipulating delays in this way is a dangerous practice as it means that sooner or later the whole system gets out of control and the turn-round time becomes four weeks instead of three, or six weeks instead of four.

There should always be a sense of urgency in decision making. The suggestor should be given the impression that the highest priority is given to all investigations and that the management will not tolerate unwarrantable delays in evaluation. Most of the large companies stress this fact in their literature about the scheme and make suggestion supervisors and administrators keep a close watch on time schedules. At Kodak it is obligatory for all reports on suggestions to be sent to the secretary within 28 days from the receipt of a copy of the suggestion. When it is not possible to make

a final report because the investigation takes longer than antici-
pated, an interim report is made stating the reasons for the delay.

The conscientious evaluator

To be effective, evaluation calls for sound technical judgment
coupled with commercial ability and a sense of fair play and
honesty. The evaluator has to believe in the suggestion scheme
and be anxious to do everything possible to encourage the workforce to participate. Bearing all this in mind it has to be realised that
the investigation has to be fitted into a busy work schedule and,
moreover, given high priority. It is hardly surprising that some
evaluators feel a certain amount of resentment; this is aggravated if
the suggestions are of low calibre and yet still call for time-
consuming investigation. If the evaluator is a conscientious and
capable person and realises the true value of the suggestion
scheme, he is more inclined to tackle the investigation with
enthusiasm than if he views the scheme with suspicion and
resentment.

To some degree therefore turn-round time depends on the type
of person who carries out the investigation and the degree of
priority he gives to the task.

Delays in processing suggestions

Evaluation, although necessarily time-consuming, represents only
one stage in the process of judging the usefulness of a suggestion.
When the evaluator has written his report it goes to the suggestion
committee for assessment and final judgment. This committee may
meet once a week, once a fortnight or, in the case of some central
committees, once a month or even once a quarter. Then again, the
time taken by the committee in making up its mind can vary quite
appreciably according to the complexity of the suggestion and the
number of reports it has to deal with at any one sitting. A works
suggestion committee meeting once a week deals with only a few
suggestions and is able to reach a decision in a fraction of the time
it takes a central committee. Moreover, the works committee has
the great advantage of being able to seek clarification on any point
arising from a suggestion from the shop floor by calling in the actual
suggestor for consultation. Supervisors and foremen should be encouraged to help workers in setting out their suggestions clearly so
that they stand the best chance of being dealt with quickly.

Cutting down on paperwork

One reason why suggestions sometimes take so long to process is that far too much paperwork is involved. One well-known engineering firm with a very healthy suggestion scheme uses twelve different forms to process a suggestion from the time it is dropped into the suggestion box to the time it reaches the suggestion committee, and each form requires several minutes to complete once all the information is at hand. Paperwork eats up time and costs a great deal of money. It is in the interests of the scheme and the company to cut out as much red tape as possible by simplifying the procedure so that the minimum number of forms are needed. Generally speaking the further the suggestion committee is removed from the actual source of suggestions, the more paperwork seems to be needed to provide the required information and the longer the turn-round time. For this reason alone a strong case can be made out for decentralisation and where possible the partial replacement of a central committee by a works/departmental committee, major suggestions only being referred to the senior body for adjudication.

Turn-round time in industrial and commercial firms

A survey of leading British companies running suggestion schemes shows that the turn-round time varies from four to ten weeks. According to the National Association of Suggestion Systems in the United States, the average processing time is given as 97 days although some firms manage to complete the work in 60–97 days depending on the complexity of the ideas being considered. There is usually a greater sense of urgency in reaching a decision in industrial companies than in commercial organisations, eg in one of the largest clearing banks the suggestion committee meets only once a quarter and in some building societies there is such a complicated procedure for evaluating suggestions via user committees and executive committees that it can take several months before a decision is reached. In Germany the processing time for suggestions rarely takes more than four weeks and some of the larger concerns manage to reduce this to three weeks.

Steps to reduce turn-round time

1. Ensure that all suggestions are clearly defined so that evaluations are carried out quickly. A great deal of time can be wasted by the

investigator in trying to understand exactly what the suggestor had in mind when he submitted his idea for an improvement. Supervisors and foremen should be encouraged to help workers in setting out their suggestions.

2. Keep a close check on the time taken by the investigator in dealing with suggestions and make sure that the agreed deadline is not exceeded, except in those rare cases where extra work had to be carried out to arrive at a fair decision.

3. Speed up the work of the suggestion committee by reducing the work-load. This can be done by delegating some of the preliminary decision making to the suggestion supervisor, administrator or works or group suggestion committees who can weed out those suggestions that are grossly unsuitable and recommend small awards for ideas of limited usefulness.

Rejections

A suggestion should never be turned down without giving adequate reasons for arriving at this decision and in all cases a letter explaining the position should be sent to the suggestor. This letter needs to be a personal one in which the suggestor is thanked for putting forward the idea and encouraged to try again (see Figure 12). It is a mistake to use a printed rejection slip as this creates a most unfavourable and unsympathetic impression. Easily the best way to handle non-adopted suggestions is by personal contact. This is the accepted practice at Perkins Engines where experience has shown that, far from being discouraged by having their ideas turned down, a high percentage of unsuccessful suggestors are only too eager to try again. The Chloride Group of Companies makes it a rule that all unsuccessful suggestors are given full details of the reasons why the suggestion committee decided not to adopt their ideas. This is the responsibility of the company's training officer who can, if requested by the suggestor, arrange for the decision of the committee to be explained to the individual concerned by the senior manager responsible for the investigation.

Re-submitting rejected suggestions

All rejected suggestions should be kept alive for a period of a year or more; the period will vary a great deal in length from company to company. Eastman Kodak keeps a suggestion in a dormant state

Mr Joesph Smith
121 Summer Street
Birmingham   February 4, 1989

Dear Mr Smith

Thank you very much for your Suggestion No. 17804. We realise that you
have spent time and effort in considering and submitting this idea and we
sincerely appreciate it.

After carefully examining your suggestion, we find that

> (*Explanation to the suggestor of why the suggestion was not accepted. This
> explanation is in detail so that there can be no misunderstanding by the
> suggestor.*)

We are sorry that this idea did not qualify for an award. However, we hope
that you will send in more suggestions in the future. A Suggestion Form is
enclosed for your convenience.

Meanwhile, if you feel that we have overlooked any of the possibilities of
your present suggestion, we invite you to discuss it with us again.

There is a one-year time limitation on suggestions. While this suggestion has
not been adopted, it will remain open for further consideration if the idea is
adopted as a result of your suggestion within one year from the date of this
letter.

Very truly yours

(*Signed*)

Chairman
Enclosure   Suggestion Committee
cc: (To Supervisor)

Figure 12: Sample 'non-adoption' letter

for seven years while General Motors gives all non-adopted
suggestions a life of one year. During the retention period the
suggestion is eligible for an award and it sometimes happens that
owing to changed conditions a suggestion which had been rejected
becomes of value and, if adopted, qualifies for an award. At the
end of the retention period the suggestion is discarded unless it
is re-submitted. This arrangement is designed to satisfy those
suggestors who think that their idea may continue to have merit
and at some future date be adopted. Occasionally this assumption
pays a dividend but in the majority of cases the rejected suggestion

dies a natural death. Most companies stipulate that suggestions must be re-submitted within a given time, usually 30 days after the retention period has elapsed. It is important that employees should be informed of any time limit on re-submissions in a letter informing them that their suggestion is not accepted.

At the end of the retention period a suggestion may be re-submitted on the standard suggestion form. Re-submitted suggestions are treated in exactly the same way as original suggestions, ie re-investigated and reconsidered by the suggestion committee. There is nothing to prevent a suggestor from re-submitting his suggestion as many times as he likes.

Reviews and re-evaluations

Inadequate initial evaluations

Where suggestions are difficult to evaluate there is always the temptation to save time and effort by recommending a minimum award in the hopes that the suggestor will be pacified and keep quiet. In the majority of cases such awards are accepted without question, but occasionally the employee requests a re-investigation. Re-investigations are always carried out much more thoroughly than original investigations and, as a result, it quite frequently happens that more favourable reports are made and more generous awards given. While this in itself provides an assurance to the suggestor that his interests are being safeguarded, it does show up a serious weakness in the scheme and clearly points to the fact that insufficient care was taken in the preliminary investigation. From the management's viewpoint this is unsatisfactory as re-investigations are expensive in time and money and add substantially to the costs of running the scheme. It is also unsatisfactory so far as the suggestor is concerned as it means that unless he challenges the preliminary findings he risks losing an award.

Appeals

If a suggestor considers that he has been unfairly treated or that some important aspect of his idea has been ignored or not properly understood, most schemes provide machinery for him to appeal. The appeal procedure varies from company to company but the normal method is for the suggestor to write to the suggestion administrator or supervisor asking for his case to be investigated and giving the reason for the request. In some companies the suggestor appeals in writing to his supervisor with a copy to the works manager. Usually a request for an appeal has to be made within the time specified in the rules and conditions governing the scheme; this can vary from one to two or more years from the date of the original submission. Where there is no recognised procedure for dealing with complaints, these are referred through the chain of command to the head of the firm or organisation, normally the managing director, for a final ruling.

Re-evaluation

Many companies make it a standard practice to review all suggestions two years after they were first considered by the suggestion committee and, where justified, to make a further award in the light of new evidence of their usefulness. A suggestion which is not adopted after this review becomes invalid and must be re-submitted as a new suggestion if the originator wants to keep the idea alive. The story of the Leva Lift clearly demonstrates this.

Alan Gair was a mechanical technician working in ICI's chemical & polymers company, Thornton Cleveleys. In his job he often had to move heavy pieces of equipment from one part of the plant to another; in particular, a special 6 cwt pump, which was constantly in use. The work of removal had to be done quickly as breakdowns meant loss of production. Removal and repair of these unwieldly pumps, which had to be manhandled, was always a rush job. Alan gave the problem a great deal of thought, drew several rough plans on the backs of envelopes and eventually made a device like a cylinder truck to move the pumps. He was not particularly proud of his effort; although it solved the immediate problem of mobility it did not provide any means of lifting the heavy piece of equipment off the ground.

Alan thought of welding a hangman's jib on the end of the truck using odd scraps of metal but his first attempts were unsuccessful as the handle bent when lifting the weight. However when a welder re-inforced the handle with more metal the problem looked as if it were solved. The pump could now be lifted without any trouble. He immediately submitted the idea to the ICI suggestion scheme. Meanwhile, back on the plant, the engineering team was still using Alan's prototype device to lift and transport pumps.

Alan's suggestion came up for review. To his great disappointment it was turned down by the works engineer on safety grounds: if the operator let go of the truck's handle it could strike him in the face and

Figure 13: The Leva Lift

might cause a serious injury. Alan lost no time in working on a modification and came up with a locking-wheel safety leg so that when released the truck remained perfectly stable. He immediately resubmitted the suggestion. He was due for yet another disappointment. The engineer was not satisfied, maintaining that the truck was still unsafe and liable to cause an accident; moreover, he issued an edict forbidding the use of the truck on the site and ordered it to be chained up out of sight.

Twelve months later the plant manager decided to refer the matter to the suggestion scheme committee and then to the board. He wanted valid reasons why Alan's truck was considered unsafe and asked that it should be properly and professionally designed by the ICI engineering design office and given a new look and identity. Alan approved of the new design. It would now lift 10 cwt instead of the original 6 and so would serve a wider purpose. The ICI suggestions committee agreed that Alan Gair should now be given his award for the idea – £2,800. This was based on the time saved in maintenance for the pump breakdowns and the cost of the loss of production outage.

This was not the end of the Leva Lift saga. The suggestions committee contacted the ICI patents department and discussed the project with a retired official who remained a good friend of the inventor. It was agreed that ICI could use the Leva Lift truck on any of their sites but they did not wish to fabricate it themselves. ICI paid for the first-year patent and agent's fees, desclaiming responsibility for the truck and reserving their right to make any trucks if they required them. Alan Gair was then introduced by the suggestion committee to Sinton Engineering who wished to manufacture the Leva Lift. This company negotiated with Alan to make ten at approximately £500 each. The inventor then visited other ICI sites throughout the country giving demonstrations of the Leva Lift's capabilities.

Pushing the invention has not been easy. Alan does, however, maintain his patent each year and recently a firm called Inventalink, who look at patent designs, contacted him with the idea of taking him as a client. A firm called Birch Engineering is also doing a market survey to see how viable the Leva Lift is likely to be.

Note: All suggestors who have ambitions to become inventors are not always treated as generously as Alan Gair. One well-known engineering company insists that the entire beneficial interest in any suggestion submitted by an employee is vested in the company. These include the rights to make applications for protection of patents for inventions in any country, and for countries abroad to claim priority under the International Convention to transfer the right to apply in any country to any third party.

7. Promotion

Although some companies maintain that a suggestion scheme has no future unless it is well supported by really aggressive publicity using every available form of promotion, there are other firms, and these include some of the most successful in the business, that believe the best way of keeping employees fully in the picture is by personal contact through first-line supervision. The Firestone Company makes wide use of supervisory personnel to conduct investigations of suggestions, and the first step is to discuss the suggestion with the employee who submitted it. In this way, employees are made to feel that the suggestion system really matters, enjoys the full support of management, and is accepted throughout the plant as the Firestone way of participating in the business.

It is important to ensure that the promotion programme is designed specifically to fit the needs of the situation. When launching a *new* suggestion system, a high pressure, all-embracing publicity campaign is essential to make sure that every employee has the right message at the right time. Timing is important, as it is no use creating interest and encouraging people to submit ideas for improvement if the administrative machinery is not ready to process the suggestions quickly and efficiently. Promoting an *established* system calls for more selective publicity aimed at bringing into the fold certain sections of the workforce where participation has fallen or where the calibre of suggestions is disappointing. Where suggestion systems show obvious signs of failure, a general review of the types of promotion already in use needs to be carried out. A new promotional campaign, if it is to be successful, must not be a re-hash of previous efforts, but should represent an entirely novel approach aimed at creating a new image and making known the many opportunities that exist for employees showing ingenuity and initiative to earn high cash awards for new ideas.

The objective of all promotional campaigns is two-fold: to achieve a higher participation rate and to obtain more ideas of real substance. Bearing this in mind, those responsible for organising the publicity should not only direct their efforts towards bringing more people into the scheme but they should be the people who are most likely to contribute worthwhile ideas which will result in substantial savings to the company.

A great deal of the success attained in publicising the scheme depends on the person chosen to do the work. Some of the most effective campaigns are carried out by suggestion co-ordinators and not by professional publicity people. The co-ordinators know the employees and how best to attract and maintain their interest. Moreover, the employees have full confidence in them. At the Firestone Company, suggestion co-ordinators are free to use all available resources, such as posters, bulletin boards, letters, press releases, media participation and, most important of all, personal contact with the staff and management so as to emphasise the importance of the company's programme.

In planning any form of publicity it has to be remembered that no matter how intelligent and forceful it may be, it cannot hope to achieve lasting results if the suggestion system is not itself firmly based on sound administrative practice. A defective administration gives rise to complaints and dissatisfaction and does a great deal of harm.

The key to success in promoting a suggestion system is to make sure that it is designed to give the maximum recognition to award winners. Recognition by the company for suggesting new ideas that cut costs and increase efficiency provides the cheapest and most effective form of promotion. Not only should the names of individuals and groups who have been successful in winning high awards be broadcast in every type of company media, but also details of the ideas that won the cash prizes. People like to know the kind of suggestions that earn good money and quite frequently a good idea helps other employees to develop promising and rewarding suggestions.

Promotion starts with the supervisory staff

Without the full co-operation of foremen and first-line supervisors, no scheme can prosper and expand. It is essential, therefore, that these men should be encouraged to sell the idea of participation to the workforce, pointing out the advantages offered by the company scheme and the kind of ideas that win major cash awards. To do this effectively, the staff needs to be continuously fed with information about the participation rate, adoption rate, percentage of high calibre ideas and the emphasis management would like to see being given to specific types of suggestions for improvements. There should be regular meetings to discuss promotion techniques and some of the problems that arise in dealing with people whose suggestions have been rejected. When the supervisory staff is made to realise that a successful suggestion system can actually make their job easier and enhance their standing in the company, they are usually only too willing to do their best to promote it.

Generation of ideas

There are many approaches to suggestion making, but one of the most productive is to take a critical look at a specific work function that needs improvement and to write down all the known factors relating to it. By analysing these facts it is often possible to think up a variety of ways to effect an improvement. The most promising of these can then be examined for defects, modified or developed after discussions with colleagues or technical experts, and finally the method chosen that has the fewest disadvantages and is the easiest and cheapest to implement. Once a problem is clearly defined, it is usually well on the way towards solution, indeed experience shows that a problem is half-solved when it is fully and properly stated.

Occasionally an idea for improvement comes as a flash of inspiration without any serious preparatory thinking, but this is the exception. In general, ideas for improvement are generated by a process of elimination and there is no easy recipe for success. It is found from experience that those closest to the work being done usually make the best suggestions for improvement. For example an electrician at the Illinois Bell Telephone Company who had long experienced trouble when using the standard pliers issued by the works store decided to redesign the tool so as to make it more nick-proof and easier to use. This man earned a merit award for the idea and recognition by the company for his initiative and ingenuity. In many cases, award-winning ideas occur because of a need to solve production problems, such as the need to make a complicated task simpler, to speed up a time-consuming job, or to cut the costs of component parts which in some manufacturers, such as motor cars, may account for 70% of total material costs.

The group approach to identifying and solving problems is now being favoured by a number of large corporations, in the United

States and in some, such as Boeing, so-called 'creativity rooms' are made available where workers can escape from the workshop atmosphere and isolate themselves in an environment that encourages the generation of ideas. To develop the group's creativity, brainstorming is often used. This well-known and well-tried technique makes possible the listing of all ideas, no matter how wild they may be. All suggestions are recorded and discussed with every member of the group taking part. Eventually, by a process of elimination, the trivial ideas are rejected and those considered worthwhile subjected to closer scrutiny until a final selection is made. The usual practice is for the group leader (generally the supervisor) to guide the discussion and control the meeting.

The problem of communication

Failure on the part of the suggestor to define clearly and concisely a problem and to state how it can be solved presents great difficulties to the administrator and evaluator who have to process the suggestion. Although it is open to those who run the scheme to refer the suggestion back to the suggestor for clarification, owing to the pressure of work and a backlog of suggestions, the suggestor is not always consulted and the result is that the suggestion is not accepted for further consideration. The suggestor's idea may be a good one but because he is unable to communicate in writing, the management misses the chance of a profitable suggestion and the employee a cash award. Unfortunately it is very difficult for some people, particularly unskilled workers, to put their thoughts on paper and failure to realise this fact is often responsible for the loss of potential money-saving ideas. Some companies encourage oral suggestions provided they are later written down on the official suggestion form. This is an excellent idea as many suggestors can, if they have a sympathetic and understanding listener, explain what they have in mind and, if the suggestion seems to have any merit, they can be helped to write it all down on paper. As the suggestion form is the cornerstone of the suggestion plan it is not possible to dispense with it, but there is no reason why oral suggestions should not be encouraged and help given where necessary in filling in the form.

At plant level at ICI every effort is made to involve the suggestor in a preliminary consideration of his idea to give him the opportunity to put his case in the best possible light. An informal meeting is arranged at which the suggestor, manager and the supervisor who will be most affected discuss the project. Usually the suggestor's shop steward is present at the meeting. ICI maintains that this informal procedure achieves the following:

1. It provides the management with the opportunity to convince the suggestor that his or her idea is being taken seriously and that, provided it shows promise, they will put it to the test in a practical and conscientious manner.
2. It involves the employee in the preliminary evaluation of his idea and gives him the chance to explain and develop the suggestion in a friendly atmosphere and on the site where it may be applied.

Promotional materials

While too much reliance should not be placed on the conventional types of promotional materials, such as explanatory booklets, posters, notices on bulletin boards, works newspapers and newsletters, these all help to stimulate interest and keep alive the company's suggestion system. Attractiveness, forcefulness and brevity are the most desirable characteristics of all these promotional tools. Booklets introducing and explaining the scheme need to be simply written, to the point, colourful and designed to make an immediate appeal. Duplicated sheets containing the same information do not have the same impact as the printed word. Money spent on producing the right kind of booklet is an investment in the future.

The ideal size for a booklet is 20cm × 10cm, preferably with a stiffish cover. The publication produced by the Ford Motor Company is a good example: it has a card cover so that it does not become dog-eared too quickly, is the right size to fit neatly in the pocket, printed in two colours, cleverly worded to hold the reader's interest and illustrated with amusing line drawings. The opening sentence commands immediate attention: 'Would you like £1,000 to spend and a new car ...?'

A number of companies give their suggestion plan leaflets catchy headings, eg Esso's compelling title, *Coin Your Ideas*, Pilkington's *Extra Cash for Extra Thought*, and IBM's *Ideas for Improvement*.

Some companies and organisations give examples of some of the ideas put forward by their employees, eg The Thames Water Ideas Group, 'Twig', has a rather novel approach. It not only sets out some of the kind of awards that the workers have achieved for good ideas illustrating them with drawings, but includes in the booklet a proposal form and simple instructions on how to go about putting forward a suggestion. The booklet, made of stiffish card, measures 20cm × 10 cm – just the right size to slip into one's pocket. The Hotpoint booklet, (14cm × 11cm) is another excellent little publication. The contents are simple and straightforward and tell the employee all he or she needs to know about the scheme. Simplicity and brevity are the most important characteristics of the most successful booklets and these are always written in a free and easy style. It should always be remembered that too many facts, piled one on top of one another, make dull reading.

Suggestion propaganda material is only useful when it is being circulated among potential suggestors. It is no use keeping stacks of booklets in store cupboards. The literature must be made to pay its way by bringing more suggestors into the scheme. People need to be constantly reminded that the system is open to bright ideas, and that these will earn recognition by the company and cash awards.

Publicity in works newspapers is a highly effective form of promotion and editors are always anxious to publish chatty news about the suggestion scheme, interviews with major award winners, features about the suggestions they made, and write-ups about presentations and other social functions held in connection with the company's suggestion system. Pictures of major award winners being presented with their cheques are always given pride of place in a works newspaper and this form of promotion pulls in more suggestors than any other feature. In Germany the Bayer Company's ten-page monthly magazine *Die Idee* is devoted entirely to news about Bayer employees who have won awards with pictures of them at work. Social functions organised in connection with the suggestion scheme are featured, also news about campaigns and other promotional efforts. Every employee at the Bayer works is given a copy of the paper.

Special campaigns

Suggestion committees are often urged by top management to embark on special campaigns to boost the adoption rate or to produce worthwhile money-saving ideas for cutting down on waste, saving energy, reducing the accident rate, etc. One of the most popular promotional techniques is the use of gifts for all employees submitting suggestions. The gifts are all low-cost items such as key-rings, cheap manicure sets, diaries, notebooks, ball-point pens, mirrors, razors, cosmetics and other toilet accessories. Some campaigns include a special lottery for first-time suggestors with quite expensive prizes such as radios and portable televisions, video equipment, record players, and watches. There are also slogan contests in which employees submit slogan ideas for improvements aimed at improving safety, cutting down waste, or quality control. There are many other similar devices to boost participation and while they often achieve an immediate return, it is doubtful if, in the long term, they are worthwhile. Such campaigns unless very carefully planned, can present serious problems. One large industrial concern handling something like a thousand suggestions a month with a participation rate of 17% embarked on a widely publicised campaign to encourage suggestions for saving energy. Within three weeks the inflow of suggestions reached 5,000. Extra staff had to be drafted into the suggestion office to handle the work and the net result in terms of ideas of real substance was disappointing, because the majority of the suggestions were quite trivial. Too large a traffic in suggestions, although gratifying from the viewpoint of statistics, means delays in processing and decision making, extra costs in running the scheme and longer turn-round time causing dissatisfaction on the shop floor. Before any campaign is launched a great deal of preliminary groundwork needs to be done so as to make certain that suggestors not only know what kind of suggestions are wanted but, of equal importance, the suggestions that are not welcome.

Suggestion days

In the United States some of the larger companies now organise special Suggestion Days for their employees in selected plants where the participation rate is dropping below the accepted norm. Inter-departmental competitions are held, with substantial prizes for the best individual and group suggestions. Prizes are also given for the highest number of suggestions adopted from a workshop or department. Lotteries are run for first-time suggestors and a banquet is organised for all employees whose suggestions have been adopted over the last six months. Events of this kind require a good deal of careful promotion in the form of posters, banners in workshops and offices, car stickers, leaflets and bulletin board notices.

Posters

To be effective, these should be bright, professionally produced and have a simple, striking message which can be readily understood. No-one stops to read a poster, it has to convey an immediate message in a flash otherwise it loses its impact. The Inland Revenue produced a colourful poster which reads: 'MIGHTY OAKS' in vivid red over a picture of a tree. At the base of the picture is the sub-title, 'Come From Little Acorns'. The simpler the story the greater the impact.

Siting is all important; a good poster can be wasted if it attracts no attention. The best positions are near entrances where there is constant traffic, in canteens, and outside rest rooms and toilets. Posters should never be allowed to stay in one position for more than a month otherwise they cease to make any impression. The help of supervisory staff should always be sought in displaying posters to the best advantage.

Presentations

The importance of recognition has been discussed above. The outstanding value of the formal presentation of awards is that it provides top management with an excellent opportunity of extending personal recognition to the employee who has contributed an idea that will benefit the company. The higher the award, the more important the occasion. Major awards should always be presented by senior managers and lesser awards by works managers or supervisors. While it can be said that each individual form of publicity plays a useful role in promoting the suggestion scheme, the culmination of all the efforts to market the system is the actual presentation of awards. This needs careful stage managing so as to make the maximum impact: presentations that are hurriedly arranged and lack the proper formality create a poor impression and miss a golden opportunity to profit fully from the occasion.

Video films

Although video films are widely used in training programmes in industry, very few companies use them for the promotion of suggestion schemes. British Rail, with its 140,000 employees, is one of the few organisations that has produced such a video. It is a very professional production with board members taking an active part in telling the BR story. It details previous ideas to the 'On Winning Lines' scheme and what happens to them after they are submitted. The climax of the video is an interview with the British Rail board member responsible for organising the BR scheme who announces that the aim is to finalise 80% of all ideas processed and evaluated within one month of being submitted. There are now a large number of companies specialising in making video films for schools and training purposes and it is well worth approaching one and discussing the project with a representative. However, beforehand it is as well to prepare a rough script outlining the kind of approach you wish to take. The film should run no longer than 15 minutes and be as straightforward as possible.

8. Union Attitudes

It would be true to say that there is no clear-cut union policy towards suggestion schemes. Throughout British industry trade union attitudes vary a great deal from company to company, and sometimes even from factory to factory within the same firm. Then again, different unions in the same company differ considerably in their reactions and it is not unusual to find one willing to support the company suggestion plan and another not prepared to take any active part in the same organisation. In some concerns shop stewards and conveners participate fully in the actual running of a suggestion scheme and do their best to encourage union members to support it. When ICI set up a working party in 1975 to re-vamp their existing scheme, shop stewards from all the divisions of the company were invited to take part. Out of a total of 19 members, 12 of these were shop stewards and only 7 were drawn from management. The present ICI scheme, which operates in all their plants, depends for its success to a large degree on union participation and where difficulties arise in running the scheme on a plant basis the men's shop stewards are always at hand to help iron out any difficulties.

Trade union attitudes towards suggestion schemes are governed largely by the climate of industrial relations that exists in the particular works. Where the horizon is darkened by threatening clouds of closures and redundancies, the prospect of active support from the unions is poor. On the other hand, where a real partnership exists between unions and management, union representatives are usually found willing to support the scheme. The position is much the same in the United States and while some companies, such as Philips Petroleum, have full union support for their suggestion system, there are many other firms in the United States where there is no union involvement. In Sweden, companies like Volvo and Saab enjoy full union co-operation and the same is true of most German firms. While union participation is highly desirable, it is not absolutely essential and there are a number of highly successful suggestion schemes where there is no union support; for example, IBM runs a very well-supported and active scheme without the presence of trade unions.

The ideal arrangement is, of course, full union co-operation making possible joint responsibility for the operation of the suggestion scheme. Union support inspires confidence and is a good insurance against failure due to lack of interest. Outright hostility towards the scheme by trade union representatives is rarely experienced and, where it does occur, it is usually due to reasons not directly connected with the scheme, eg the introduction of new codes of practice dictated by new technologies.

It has to be remembered that the main concern of the unions in every business is to look after employees' wages and conditions of employment, and they tend to regard exercises such as suggestion schemes, as fringe activities outside their sphere of responsibility. In a way this is a logical and understandable attitude provided the union's negative attitude does not influence the acceptance of the scheme by the workforce. In many cases the unions are prepared to stand on the touch line and see fair play for their members, and to act in their true capacity as negotiators in securing better treatment for members who have a grievance against the suggestion committee or administrator.

In general, it is perhaps true to say that trade unions regard suggestion schemes with some suspicion and uneasiness. The reasons can best be summarised as follows:

1. Fear that suggestion schemes and allied forms of incentive devices in which employees are encouraged to become more closely involved in the company's business tend to draw the workers' allegiance away from the union and towards the employer. This tends to weaken the hold they have over their members. ·
2. Fear that the kind of cost-cutting suggestions the management is looking for must inevitably lead to greater mechanisation of processes and procedures. In making suggestions leading to greater productivity the workers are, some unions claim, suggesting themselves out of a job.
3. Fear that as the traditional type of suggestion scheme is based on an individual award for adopted ideas it makes too great an appeal to the worker's self-interest and self-satisfaction, and tends to weaken the team spirit. This is contrary to the declared union policy which is aimed at strengthening team spirit.
4. Fear that incentive schemes, such as the suggestion plan, help to create a more settled and stable attitude to work and, as a result, workers are less willing to take any disruptive action that will interfere with their ordered way of life.
5. Fear that employees are being imposed upon by employers to supply potentially valuable ideas at a cut price. Unions maintain that if

managements were obliged to buy some of these ideas outside, say from consultants, they would have to pay the market price which would bear no relation to the paltry sums paid to suggestors.

While most of these fears are groundless, some of them stem from a natural anxiety and responsibility to look after the interests of the workers. The unions are apprehensive about technological change because of its effect on employment. They realise only too well that as the pace of industrial change quickens many of the old skills acquired by their members over long years of service will no longer be in demand and this applies not only in the manufacturing industries but in many clerical and administrative operations. No matter how one disguises the fact, by encouraging employees to put forward ideas for improvement, the employer is encouraging a new attitude towards change and a willingness to accept change in every type of operation.

It is no exaggeration to say that the unions react strongly to any move that threatens their authority by bypassing and undermining the traditional trade union structure. In many cases union opposition to management's proposals for change is inspired not so much by the nature of the change – for example, process automation now accepted by the workforce in many chemical and oil refining factories – but by the way in which it is introduced. Underlying the unfavourable attitude of the unions towards the suggestion scheme is the feeling that it is a management device to increase productivity and solve quality problems without making use of the recognised union negotiating procedure.

To allay some of the fears of the unions that suggestion systems are aimed primarily at job elimination or downgrading, every effort should be made by management to stress the fact that labour- and time-saving ideas are designed to make a more efficient use of labour and to increase efficiency, thereby increasing profitability and improving the competitiveness of the company. A good deal of the friction caused by technological change is due to a failure on the part of employers to communicate and consult with the unions before actually making decisions on the installation of new plant, new processes and procedures which are likely to alter the whole pattern of manpower distribution. A successful American example of a joint union/management suggestion scheme is described in Appendix B.

9. Quality Circles

In recent years much publicity has been given to 'quality circles' which originated in Japanese industry after the Second World War. Employees learn how to solve problems in manufacture and commerce, develop new projects in scientifically ordered ways and come thoroughly involved in the company's business, using several well established techniques, such as brainstorming, cause and effect diagrams, Pareto diagrams, histograms, check sheets, graphs and case studies.

Essentially 'quality circles' are an attempt to involve the workforce more closely with the products they are producing by improving and maintaining quality standards and encouraging suggestions on working practices and systems. To some extent therefore they draw on the experience of and share some of the characteristics and problems associated with the more traditional type of suggestion scheme. When quality circle activities are carried out in firms operating the traditional suggestion scheme, it has been found that they have a positive effect on the scheme and enhance its value.

Quality circles have been taken up by every kind of business from steel rolling mills to dress design and manufacture, and all types of employee from senior managers to the rank and file, from engineers and design departments through purchasing to sales. The subjects of study undertaken are highly diversified; in large manufacturing concerns problems relating to quality control probably account for 50% of time, productivity problems and cost reduction 40%, safety and others 10%.

It is interesting to note that the idea was based on statistical methods of quality control introduced by the American occupation forces in Japan during the immediate post-war years. The first determined effort made by the Japanese government to break away from the 'poor quality' image of pre-war Japanese goods was the passing of the Industrial Standardisation Law in 1949. From this government-inspired drive to improve the quality of manufactured goods the idea of developing quality control as a new kind of work discipline was soon taken up on a nation-wide scale. By 1962 most of the large companies in Japanese industry had formed quality circles and were busy training supervisors and foremen in the new skills. Since that time fantastic growth has been experienced and today there are more than half a million circles operating with five million members. There is a national organisation which monitors progress, registers circle workers and every year holds a national Quality Control Circle Conference at which all the leading companies report their activities.

Quality circle activities and suggestion programmes often run side by side. In the Toyota Motor Company 527,717 suggestions were submitted in 1978, 86% of these were adopted and about $2.5 million awarded to workers. Savings to the company during that period exceeded the figure by five or six times.

Membership of quality circles is voluntary, although, in the early days some Japanese firms applied pressure to persuade employees to join circles. A circle is made up of 10–14 people and the generally accepted practice is to have employees who normally work together and know one another's qualifications and experience. Rank and file members of a circle meet two or four times a week or, in some firms, twice a month, in their own time for one or two hours in rooms set aside for the purpose and away from the hurly-burly of everyday work. Each meeting is chaired by a foreman or supervisor, known as the leader, who has been specially trained in problem-solving techniques by a qualified quality control engineer. The function of the leader is to see that the special techniques used in problem solving are applied with the most effect and that the group is taken through each stage with every member taking an active part in the discussions.

The way a circle meeting is conducted varies a good deal from company to company, but it is vitally important that each individual is made to feel that he is able to influence decisions and to participate fully in problem solving. Senior managers usually meet once a month to review their own jobs and to consider ways of improving their work performance. Not all companies use the recognised orthodox approach to problem solving; some have evolved their own methods which they apply with great success. The final result is the same, however, that is the workforce becomes fully involved in problem solving. Although the management is directly responsible for organising quality circle activities, it remains aloof from the actual working of a circle and refrains from telling the members what to do and what not to do. It must be stressed though that the whole success of the quality circle concept depends on the interest and enthusiasm shown by management in the development and application of quality circle activities throughout the company.

A quality circle meeting needs to be carefully planned before-hand and the plan, once made, meticulously followed. The basic tools of analysis, such as Pareto analysis, control charts, etc, must be fully utilised and the whole operation carried out scientifically. The first objective is to discover and carefully define the problems to be studied. They can be of a general nature, such as how to increase the productivity of a unit or to reduce maintenance, or they may be specific problems relating to a particular machine or process. Suggestions may be put forward by the leader or by members. Usually there is no lack of known production problems but, where these cannot be readily identified, then brainstorming is a well recognised method of bringing ideas to the surface.

Having identified a problem, the next stage is to discover the underlying causes responsible for its occurrence. Here it is useful to develop a cause-and-effect diagram so as to discover systema-tically what the causes are. Following this the group has to try and isolate the causes in order of importance by collecting and analys-ing data. The development of counter-measures to correct the causes then follows. Various improvement procedures are recom-mended, most of them consisting of simple questionnaires:

1. Why is it necessary?
2. What is its purpose?
3. Where should it be done?
4. When should it be done?
5. Who should do it?
6. How should it be done?

The next logical step is to put into force the corrective measures suggested and to check the results. If the results are not satisfac-tory the work must be done all over again. Once it is confirmed that a solution to the problem has been found that meets all practical requirements, then a report has to be written and pre-sented to the management for approval. Once it is approved the new procedure is adopted as standard practice.

It needs to be emphasised that quality circles provide a framework into which many different techniques can be fitted. Algorithms, now well established as a means of plotting the strategy of problem solving in computers, can be used as a tool in solving problems in industry and even in detecting faults in machinery. New tech-niques, such as Simplex Evolutionary Operation or EVOP, can also be used very effectively for solving productivity problems not only in the process industries but in manufactures using traditional batch processes.

Summing up, it can be said that quality control circles provide the employer with a simple, logical approach to problem solving that involves the workforce in the actual mechanics of the operation. Not only are they effective in achieving improvements in productivity and cost cutting, which makes a worthwhile contribution to the prosperity and competitiveness of the company, but they provide employees with new opportunities to participate in the firm's business.

It has been said that the main reason for the phenomenal success of quality control in Japan was the early discovery and appreciation of each worker's dignity and creativity, and a full realisation of the importance of his participation in problem solving which, prior to the introduction of quality control, had always been looked upon as a management responsibility. There are, of course, problems in applying the concept to industry in the West because of the western worker's resistance to discipline, his distrust of participation and natural reluctance to abide by decisions made by a consensus of opinion. However, from experience gained in the United States, where several of the large corporations have taken up the idea, it would appear that quality circle activities can be adapted to suit western needs and western workers. Success would seem to be assured once the idea is enthusiastically supported by top management and leaders are properly trained in the various problem-solving techniques used in Japanese industry. While it is doubtful whether the quality circle way of industrial life as practised in Tokyo would ever apply in quite the same way in Akron or Manchester, there is no doubt that a great deal would be gained not only in material prosperity but in industrial relations by helping to break down the barriers between 'them' and 'us'.

It has to be remembered that in most quality control activities in Japan the emphasis is on non-monetary awards such as recognition and job satisfaction. However, some companies do pay their quality control circles for solutions producing worthwhile savings and others run traditional suggestion plans alongside their quality control operations.

There is no doubt that the quality circle concept is capable of being adapted to meet many of the needs of modern industry which only now is beginning to realise that the workforce can, if given the right kind of encouragement and training, make great contributions to the well-being and competitiveness of the company.

10. Conclusions: The key to a Successful Scheme

The essential elements of a successful suggestion scheme can best be summarised as follows:

- Strong management support;
- Recognition of award winners;
- Continuous promotion of the scheme;
- Equitable award system; and
- Union involvement where practicable.

Experience has shown that two other factors are also of crucial importance: decentralisation and delegation of authority, and the appointment of effective plant representatives. Most of the large companies with factories spread over the country now delegate the responsibility for running their suggestion schemes to plant managements. In the United States this policy is regarded as standard practice, for example, Du Pont maintains that each site should be responsible for co-ordinating its own scheme.

Hoechst in Frankfurt has had many years' experience in running a suggestion scheme. The conditions it considers essential for a successful system are very similar to those above:

1. An enthusiastic manager, expert in his field, as motivator.
2. Careful preparation.
3. Tactical procedure.
4. Up-to-date organisation: board/committee guidelines, registration.
5. Rapid processing.
6. Adequate awards.
7. Stimulating promotional material.

The first three points can be regarded as 'personal conditions', the last four as 'functional conditions'.

Management support

Strong management support is essential for the healthy growth of a suggestion scheme. Lack of interest by top management filters down through all branches of the organisation and is eventually reflected in a dwindling participation rate and a lowering of the quality of suggestions submitted by employees. It is the responsibility of senior management to ensure that the promotion and operation of the scheme is accepted as an integral part of management duties. The lower echelons of management must be totally committed to the scheme and prepared to work alongside the administrator or suggestion supervisor. Line supervisors need to be made accountable for any falling off of employee interest.

Management involvement can take several forms: one of the most effective is for departmental heads to set specific goals in their own departments and to take a day-to-day interest in the progress of the scheme and the success achieved by the staff in reaching their objectives. Evaluation and assessment of suggestions should be as close to the suggestor and his work group as possible. Every effort should be made to involve the suggestor in the investigation and evaluation at some stage, eg consulting him to clear up any queries regarding the practicality of his idea. Competition also injects life into a job and stimulates production. It has been demonstrated repeatedly that when an employee or group of employees competes, performance is better than if no competition or rivalry is involved.

Recognition of award winners

Senior management should demonstrate its commitment to the scheme by public recognition of the individual or department responsible for a successful suggestion. Recognition should be regarded as the cornerstone of every scheme as it is one of the surest ways of motivating employees to think creatively about production problems. By giving praise, credit and publicity to suggestions of outstanding merit, not only is the suggestor who is responsible gratified and encouraged to submit more and better ideas in the future, but his friends and workmates are stimulated to follow suit. Recognition of employees' achievements by management reflects credit on the supervisor, adds to his personal prestige and standing in the eyes of his staff and, what is of greater significance, closely identifies the company with the scheme. In many cases, recognition is a more powerful force than monetary award. Acknowledgement of achievement calls for careful planning and skilful stage managing so as to secure the greatest impact.

Continuous promotion

Unless the supervisory staff make an all out effort to interest their workforce in the suggestion scheme by telling them of the opportunities that exist for good ideas to boost production and cut costs, and to help them in putting their ideas forward, then the participation rate is unlikely to increase. Selling the suggestion scheme to employees is a continuous job and one in which both management and supervisors are closely involved. It is management's responsibility to make sure that the supervisor understands what is wanted and why, and that the workforce knows what is happening and is never made to feel remote from the policy-makers. By putting forward ideas which contribute to the prosperity of the company, employees can become more closely involved in its affairs.

Suggestions of real substance which result in appreciable savings to the company form only a small percentage of those dropped into the box, the vast majority of acceptable ideas are relatively simple ones leading to minor improvements and small savings. First-time suggestors rarely come up with outstanding ideas, and experience tends to show that third and fourth-time suggestors, the real triers, are usually the ones who come up with the best ideas. It is, therefore, important for the future of the scheme that first-timers whose ideas have not been accepted should be looked upon as potentially valuable members of the company's thinking team and given every encouragement to persevere and try again. One sure way to win the allegiance of the unsuccessful suggestor is to make sure that someone in authority talks to him and explains where the initial attempt went wrong and why he should keep on trying.

Rejection of suggestions should be handled with the greatest care. The word 'rejected' should never be used; terms such as 'not adopted' or 'not accepted' are preferable. In all cases where a suggestion is not accepted, the reasons should be explained to the suggestor by the administrator or supervisor in person. Where a personal interview is not possible then a carefully worded letter should be sent, giving the reasons why the idea cannot be accepted. Every effort should be made to ensure that the sugestor is encouraged to try again.

Equitable award system

The scale of payments for worthwhile suggestions should bear some relation to the value which the employer attaches to them in the form of actual savings or intangible benefits. A fair award system that represents a reasonable return to the suggestor provides a clear indication that the company considers the scheme to be important and worthy of support. Generous payments for good ideas attract a flow of high calibre suggestions, whereas mean awards provide no incentive and produce a trickle of mediocre ideas. It is important that the scale of payments for suggestions should be adjusted every two or three years to keep abreast of inflation and changing conditions.

A frequent criticism of many schemes is that awards are either inadequate or the method of calculating them so complicated that no-one can understand it. As a result the shop-floor worker begins to mistrust the system and thinks that the firm is trying to get new ideas for improvement on the cheap.

Union co-operation

Fortunately, outright union opposition to a company suggestion scheme is rare; in most organisations the union's attitude is one of indifference. Shop stewards, whilst not condemning the venture, show little inclination to become involved. However, there is no doubt that a suggestion plan enjoys wider acceptance by the workforce if union representatives give it their support. Every effort should be made by management to persuade union representatives to co-operate by helping in the actual running of the scheme – if possible, by persuading the works convener to become a member of the suggestion committee.

The job environment

To be successful a scheme, whether operated by a bank or an engineering workshop, has to be sufficiently adaptable to meet rapidly changing conditions and appeal to different sets of people. New opportunities are constantly being opened up. During recent years there has been an upsurge of interest in revitalising schemes to give them a modern image and make them better suited to the conditions imposed by new technologies. In the United States blue-collar workers are a shrinking minority of the workforce (33%) and white-collar workers have become an outright majority (51%). This is a highly significant change and has to be considered when drawing up the rules and conditions governing a scheme. In addition the growing trends towards participative management with changes in the traditional supervisor-subordinate relationship means that schemes have to be restructured to take account of new methods of management. Radical changes in the character of the work carried out in a department may also necessitate alterations; for example, where the office services department in a large commercial organisation is converted to a modern data processing division run by a younger staff.

In industry today the great emphasis is on the introduction of new systems that will make possible reductions in staff, greater throughput and higher quality control. While it would be unrealistic to think that suggestion schemes can make the life of middle management any easier, at least they will open the door to bright ideas for solving some of the problems facing employees who have to adapt themselves to the new order of things. Whereas in the early days of most schemes, managements were satisfied with ideas of a simple nature calling for minor modifications to equipment, today it is realised that schemes can be widened to encourage more ambitious ideas that offer the prospect of larger savings. This is possible if the scope of a scheme is broadened to bring in the lower echelons of management with their more specialised knowledge and experience.

Another important requirement for success is good worker morale; schemes will only achieve minimal success if morale is not reasonably high. It has been noted that in those firms where the 'superior-subordinate syndrome' is avoided and two-way communication ensured, there is a high rate of participation in suggestion schemes. Once a job is made interesting by cross-training and diversifying skills, and by job enrichment which gives more responsibility, there is a greater awareness of the obstacles that stand in the way of progress and an increased readiness to help find solutions to current problems. Once everyone knows what is expected and goals are set which are realistic, personal, specific and involve people not mere statistics, a new interest in problem solving is awakened.

The Japanese ensure full co-operation from their workers by demonstrating the company's total commitment to them by open management with proper consultation. This policy is now being followed by some of the large American corporations. The Boeing Company, which has the highest dollar return on awards given (in excess of $16 million for four locations), attributes its success to the high morale of its workforce and the creation of a working environment that is conducive to optimum productivity.

Although it has long been recognised that keeping the worker informed of what is happening around him is a difficult and often thankless task, it is essential if his help is to be recruited in solving factory-floor problems. Some workers do not want to become involved in company business and the unions are often either indifferent or antagonistic towards employee participation. However, there is a growing body of workers who are conscious of the benefits that can be derived from participation in the form of cash awards for ideas leading to improvements. Building up the worker's interest in the job is the first step towards encouraging him to start asking questions, such as:

- Is there a better way or a quicker way of doing the job?
- Can the efficiency of the operation be improved?
- Is there a way of preventing waste, cutting costs and saving time?
- Can the operation be made safer?

A machine operator at Perkins Engines, who ranks as one of the top suggestors in the country, says that he has learned never to take anything for granted just because it is there. He queries things, and if he can see a way of saving time or material, he puts his proposal forward. The worker has to be made to understand that it is well worth his while to think up new ideas for improving his job in terms of cash, job satisfaction and recognition. These are solid enough advantages to start most thinking men and women on the road to creative thinking.

Companies need to ensure that employees with ideas for improvement are not discouraged by early failures. Where suggestions fall short because they have not been properly thought out, management should endeavour to provide information and facilities to convert the germ of a good idea into a workable and useful proposal that will earn the person a handsome award. The Bayer Company is one well-known firm that offers practical help to develop workers' ideas for improvement provided they show promise and when developed will increase productivity and cut costs.

Reasons for breakdown of schemes

As a generalisation it can be said that the breakdown of a suggestion plan is seldom due to a single cause. Lack of proper direction and clear aims and objectives certainly increases the risk of a scheme's failure to attract a reasonable percentage of ideas of substance. Employees must know what kind of ideas the company is trying to attract and the channels of communication must be kept open between management and workforce.

In order to clarify their objectives, companies intending to introduce a suggestion scheme, should perhaps follow the example of British Telecom and set out the main objectives as they apply to the company and its employees.

When British Telecom started to revise the 1984 suggestion scheme in 1988 they had three clearly defined goals. First, to make an important and positive contribution to staff morale; second, to increase profitability; third, and most important, to make possible quality improvement. The company had invested in a comprehensive training package called 'total quality management', already tried and tested by Rank Xerox, which drives home the need for an employee to 'own' a project and not to pass the buck. BT had every confidence in achieving full co-operation from the workforce.

The detailed objectives of the new British Telecom scheme may be set out as follows:

1. To harness the creativity and talent of all UKC managers and staff
2. To recognise and equably reward adopted ideas and to encourage ideas resulting from careful thought even if not adopted
3. To ensure that awards fairly reflect the value of the idea to BT/UKC and are of sufficient level to stimulate further ideas
4. To run, throughout the business, a consistent and well managed scheme in which it is easy to participate
5. Each UKC unit was required to achieve the following response rates:

   One idea per 75 employees by December 1988

   One idea per 40 employees by December 1989

   One idea per 20 employees by December 1990
6. Each UKC unit to measure its implementation rate and seek to achieve a success rate of:

   35 per cent implementation of ideas submitted by December 1988

   40 per cent implementation of ideas submitted by December 1989

   50 per cent implementation of ideas submitted by December 1990

In a very comprehensive review of the scheme it was stressed that visible support and involvement by senior management was the main enabling factor; every effort was made to make managers feel that their contribution was vital to the overall success of the scheme.

To many shop-floor workers, the submission of a suggestion is rather an ordeal, calling for much thought and effort. Once the completed form has been dropped in the box or forwarded to the suggestion office via the internal mail, the suggestor is impatient to know how his idea has been received by the management. Most employees are reasonable people and do not expect to know whether their brain-child has been accepted or rejected in a day or so, but long delays stretching into several weeks or months are inexcusable and seriously prejudice the future of the scheme. Immediate acknowledgement of the suggestion is essential and should be followed up by personal contact with someone in the suggestion office, who can explain the steps that are being taken to consider his idea carefully before arriving at any decision.

Unnecessary delay in decision making is responsible for more complaints than any other factor and is a major reason for a low participation rate. In America the average processing time for suggestions varies from 30 to 90 days. British turn-round time is more or less on a par with these figures, although some companies manage to complete the operation in three weeks.

A suggestion scheme will also lose credibility when suggestions which have received awards are not implemented, or if suggestions rejected in one plant are later found to be adopted and in use in another plant or department.

Summary

1. Adequate resources in the form of skilled personnel, accommodation and other services to operate and administer the scheme properly. To try and run a suggestion scheme on the cheap is a certain recipe for failure.
2. Provision of generous awards for ideas of real substance.
3. Personal recognition of all award winners by top management.
4. Minimum turn-round time.
5. Involvement of the suggestor in the evaluation of his scheme.
6. Involvement of unions in running the scheme, preferably by the presence of the works convener on the suggestions committee. Union involvement gives the scheme prestige and helps to inspire confidence in the way it is being administered.
7. Full supporting publicity. Many suggestion schemes fade away after a few years because they have not been kept alive by adequate promotion.
8. Explanation to the suggestor of reasons for rejection of his idea.

Appendix A Suggestion Schemes for Management

In many companies in the manufacturing and process industries management grades are excluded from the suggestion scheme for payroll workers. The fallacy of this policy is now being realised by some firms and they have devised special suggestion programmes for the lower echelons of management. The supervisory grades in any business have an unequalled knowledge and experience of working processes and procedures, and these are the employees who are most likely to be able to contribute ideas of real substance.

The Vauxhall 'Management Cost Suggestion Programme' is devised and operated for foremen and supervisors up to and including eighth level. The proposals for improvements submitted under this scheme must be outside the employee's job and responsibilities; ideas are not accepted that deal with personnel safety or the day-to-day running of the suggestor's own group or department. Suggestions are evaluated on a point basis eg Vauxhall gives three points for all accepted studies plus one point per £100 saved or part of, up to a maximum of 100 points for each proposal. Each of these Vauxhall points is worth 500 award credits for which goods and services can be obtained from an outside agency. The scheme does not provide for cash awards (see Figures 14 and 15).

In addition to the points gained by any one individual for which he can, of course, obtain selected merchandise or services, all those who have gained points qualify for competitions which are held yearly to find the best individual in the company and he is awarded tokens to the value of £750. The runners-up, the best individuals in each of the other plants, each win £500 in award tokens.

The goods and services which are available cover a wide field and include clothing, jewellery, home and office equipment, etc. Some of the items listed in the agency's catalogue require a large number of credits, eg a fur coat needs 119,120 award credits.

The Vauxhall 'Management Cost Suggestion Programme' also provides several opportunities for social functions; for example, foremen from the best division in each plant every year are invited to a celebration dinner-dance with their wives at which members of management are present.

G45-3

FOR OFFICE USE

DATE	REFERRED TO

MANAGEMENT COST STUDY PROGRAMME

FILE COPY

FOR OFFICE USE: COST STUDY NO.

DATE REC'D.

PLEASE PRINT CLEARLY THROUGHOUT USING HARD PENCIL OR BALL-POINT PEN

NAME:	DEPARTMENT	ROUTE No.	OCCUPATION

PLEASE GIVE ALL THE FOLLOWING DETAILS WHERE APPLICABLE.

PART NAME:	PART No.	MODELS:	STANCHION No.	BUILDING No.
MACHINE NAME:	TOOL/MACHINE No.	OPERATION No.		

SUBJECT ....

DETAILS OF PRESENT METHOD/DESIGN/EQUIPMENT ....

....

....

....

PROPOSAL FOR IMPROVEMENT:

....

....

....

....

....

....

....

....

....

....

....

....

(Do not write on any other page or on the reverse of this form. If more space is required you may use a further set).

This Cost Study is submitted for consideration under the terms and conditions of the Vauxhall Cost Study Programme as set out on the reverse side of acknowledgement. I understand and agree that Vauxhall Motors Ltd., General Motors Corporation and its subsidiaries, successors and assigns shall have the right to make full use of my study.

SIGNATURE(S) .... **DATE** ....

If you would prefer no publicity put X here ☐

DO NOT DETACH ANY COPIES   SEND COMPLETED FORM TO SUGGESTIONS DEPT., LUTON 7938 or E. PORT 394

FOR OFFICE USE ONLY:		CONSIDERED BY COMMITTEE:	
DATE	CHAIRMAN	AWARD	CHECKED

REFER TO BACK OF FORM FOR RULES OF THE VAUXHALL COST STUDY PROGRAMME

Figure 14: A management cost study form

RULES APPLYING TO
MANUFACTURING COST
STUDIES

A STUDY is a proposal to improve something in a specified manner. Studies are submitted by Management staff on G45/3 forms available from Suggestions Department. Completed Study forms are posted via internal mail system, routing for studies is Luton 7938, Ellesmere Port 394.

1.   FUNCTION OF THE COMMITTEE

The Committee determines:

(a)   Whether employees are eligible to receive points for adopted studies

(b)   Whether studies are eligible for points consideration

(c)   The number of points awarded paid for adopted cost studies.

2.   ELIGIBLE EMPLOYEES

All members of Management up to 8th level inclusive are eligible to participate, when their proposals are outside the scope of their regular job assignment, or their departments responsibilities. Assignments in conjunction with other departments are not eligible subjects for cost study submissions.

3.   ELIGIBLE STUDIES

(a)   All studies proposing to improve something in a specified manner are eligible for award consideration except those pertaining to the following:

(i)   Appearance changes in the product, for appearance reasons only

(ii)   Modification to tools and equipment used by Salvage Groups on salvage rework or operations where no planning exists.

(iii)   Ideas, methods or equipment already under consideration or development

(iv)   Routine maintenance or repair matters and safety items

(v)   Minor errors in drawings and instructions

(vi)   Matters of Company policy, or matters governed by contracts with others

(vii)   Advertising or public relations matters

(viii)   Employee discounts and employee relations matters

(ix)   Recreation Club and Canteen matters

(x)   Housekeeping

(b)   Studies relating to a production model are not eligible for consideration until that model is released to production.

(c)   Studies relating to sheet or coil blank sizes are not eligible for consideration until a minimum of four production runs have been completed, or the part has been in production a minimum of two months, which ever is the later

(d)   Studies relating to sheet or coil material grade are not eligible for consideration until one production run has been made using the material shown on the Manufacturing Specification.

(e)   Cost Studies pertaining to alternative uses for parts or material not in current use are not eligible for consideration unless the recognised investigation procedure for such parts/material has been carried out and a Surplus Material Disposal Tag issued.

(f)   Should a cost study not be adopted within one year following the date of the non-adoption, it will receive no further consideration, unless within 30 days following the one year period the suggestor

requests in writing that the suggestion be held open for an additional one year period.

In this case the earlier study will be eligible for award consideration if adopted during the additional one year period.

(g)   When two employees have signed a cost study which is adopted, any points are divided equally between them.

4.
All decisions by the Cost Study Committee are final. However, if at any time a supervisor wishes to re-open a study to present new or additional information, the Committee at its discretion may review its decision.

5.
No more than two people may combine to put forward a study.

6.
A study must always be written out on a cost study form and submitted to the Suggestions Office before any action is taken to implement the idea. No unauthorised modifications, alterations, or deletions to machinery, equipment, plant or components may be undertaken in order to try out a study. The proposer(s) must sign the cost study.

7.
The Company reserves the right to terminate or vary the programme on giving reasonable notice of its intentions to do so.

8.
A cost study made under the terms and conditions of the Vauxhall Motors Cost Study Programme is not made in confidence and Vauxhall Motors Limited, General Motors Corporation and its subsidiaries, and their assigns shall not be obligated in any way with respect to such proposals except as provided under the Rules of the Programme.

9.
Depending on the nature of his employment, an employee submitting cost study under the Vauxhall Motors Cost Study Programme maybe free to seek patent protection to his proposal, but any protection he may obtain shall be subject to the right granted on the reverse side to Vauxhall Motors Limited, General Motors Corporation and its subsidiaries, and their successors and assigns to make full use of his cost study.

AWARDS

10. (a)   The minimum award for an accepted study is three points

(b)   The maximum award for an accepted study is 100 points

(c)   Points are totalled for an operational year, to decide :

(a)   Individual Company Champion, who is the person with most points achieved in the year period concerned.

(b)   Plant Champion (as above)

(d)   The Company Champion wins special prize of token to be used for goods, value £750.

(e)   Plant Champions win token as above, value £500.

(f)   Luton, Dunstable, Ellesmere Port and Central Staff, are to be considered as individual Plants, i.e. four in total.

(g)   Supervisors etc. of the best department in each Plant, are invited (with their wives) to a dinner dance. Senior members of Management will attend. All 100 point winners are invited regardless of department. The best department is decided by dividing the total points scored by eligible people, in that department, during that year, by the number of eligible people in the department. The Cost Study year is from 1st January to 31st December

All Vauxhall points are converted and issued in the form of certificates, which are used for goods chosen from a prize catalogue.

Figure 15: Rules for cost study

The Ford Motor Company in the United States operates a suggestion plan for salaried employees in the executive, supervisory and administrative branches. There are six levels of awards for original ideas that go beyond the normal requirements of the employee's job and that will save money or improve working conditions or product quality. The top award for a proposal calculated to save the company $25,000 or more is a car, or some other company product. Suggestors may also receive their award in US Savings Bonds. (It should be noted here that the value of the car or other goods is regarded by the US Revenue as income and is subject to tax which is normally deducted from the employee's regular salary.)

Appendix B A Joint Union-Management Suggestion Plan

The Beech Aircraft Company of Wichita, Kansas, makes a wide range of aircraft and computer equipment for the aircraft industry, it is highly successful and employs 10,500 people. Before January 1976 it ran a conventional suggestion scheme which both management and union felt was not making any significant contribution to productivity because of its failure to attract sufficient high calibre ideas for improvement. The union was particularly critical of the management-run scheme which, they said, was missing out on a potential gold mine of workers' suggestions.

As a result of negotiations with the union, the management decided to introduce a radically different type of jointly-sponsored suggestion plan, in which the workers would be fully involved and control placed in the hands of a joint company/union negotiating committee made up of five management representatives and eight union men.

It was proposed that the actual running of the new scheme should be left to a productivity council made up of 300 elected shop-floor representatives. The distribution of these representatives throughout the plant was arranged on a geographical as well as a functional basis so that on average there would always be one council representative for every 30 workers. The function of council members was to promote interest in the scheme and actively assist workers in developing new ideas for increasing productivity, cutting costs, improving safety, reducing waste, quality control and labour saving.

All employees of the company were invited to take part in the plan; the only people excluded were corporate officers and the supervisory staff responsible to the productivity council for administering the scheme. The whole operation was designed to enable any employee with a promising idea to be given every help in developing it into a practical, money-saving suggestion. The day-to-day working of the Beechcraft scheme follows three basic stages which are summarised below.

1. Once an employee has thought of an idea he discusses it with his council representative who helps to work it out in detail so that it becomes a concrete proposal suitable for setting out on a proposal form. Within five days of completing the form a member of the council and an evaluator meet the worker, discuss the idea and give him a typed copy of the proposal. On the first Tuesday after the employee has been contacted, the proposal is considered by the suggestor's foreman or supervisor, a council representative and a member of the productivity council staff. These men look at the suggestion in the light of three basic questions:
   - Is the idea practical?
   - Does it offer savings in productivity in any form, such as time or dollar savings, less waste, greater safety, improved quality, etc?
   - Will the proposal as submitted stand a reasonable chance of being adopted and put into practice?

   If two of the three members present at the meeting answer 'Yes' to these three questions the committee has the authority to award an early recognition award of $10. (This is merely a form of saying 'Thank you' for taking part in the plan.)
2. Once the proposal has been accepted by the committee, it is assigned to an expert, a member of the resource panel, whose responsibility it is to see that the suggestion is promptly and thoroughly investigated and evaluated. The result is then sent to the productivity council for final appraisal of the proposal's worth in terms of first year's savings to the company.
3. When a proposal has been accepted, it goes before the weekly meeting of the recognition group within the council which recommends which proposals should be considered for an award. The manager has the authority to award $20 to each suggestor whose idea has been accepted but is not of sufficient merit to justify any further award. These 'manager awards' are intended to reward employees for suggestions which in the old scheme would have gone unrecognised. The remaining proposals are submitted anonymously to the monthly meeting of a combined company/union recognition committee for review and final evaluation. This committee can award any proposal sums from $30 to $100. All proposals receiving $30 to $50 are officially closed, while those in the higher bracket are held open for further assessment. This final assessment which takes place twice a year is carried out by a special review committee made up of company and union oficials. It takes a closer look at all the ideas and decides which of them qualify for higher awards ranging from $100 to $1,000. Once these awards are paid the proposals are closed. The entire procedure is summarised in Figure 16.

Apart from increases in productivity resulting from implementing workers' suggestions, the Beechcraft suggestion plan has made possible a marked improvement in employee attitudes towards their work which in itself often leads to secondary productivity increases. Both management and union agree that since the scheme was introduced workers have been more contented, labour relations have improved, morale is good and absenteeism reduced. From a profitability angle the company is well satisfied with the results and reports a return of four-to-one on investment. About 800–900 ideas for improvement are received every month and half of them are adopted for use.

One outstanding advantage of the new plan over the conventional type of suggestion scheme is that the employee is heavily involved from the moment he discusses his idea with the council representative to the time he is told the final decision of the evaluator. Moreover, by being given the opportunity of serving as a productivity council representative, he participates fully in the running of the scheme.

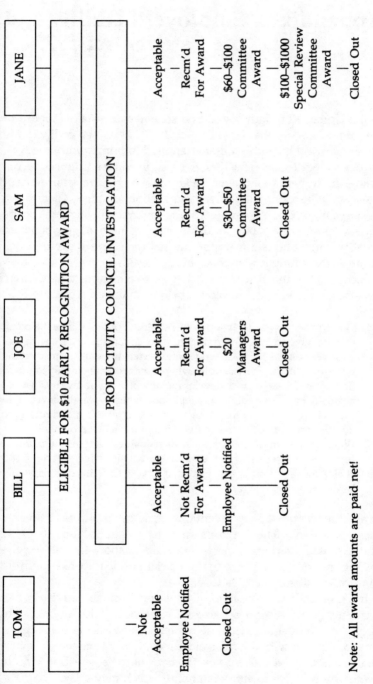

Note: All award amounts are paid net!

Figure 16: Suggestion handling procedures

Appendix C Employer Liability and the Patents Act 1977

In the United Kingdom suggestion schemes must take account of the provisions of the Patents Act 1977. This Act codified the existing law on the subject and attempted to bring it into line with European legislation. The 1977 Act also introduced clauses recognising the rights of employee inventors which have an important effect on all those involved with suggestion schemes. Clearly not all suggestions can be patented or are inventions within the scope of the Patents Act, but in those cases where suggestions do constitute inventions it is important that the scope and provisions of the Act are fully understood and followed.

Section 39 of the Patents Act defines two circumstances where inventions made by an employee belong to the employer:

1. When in the course of an employee's normal duties – or as the result of being given a special assignment – the circumstances are such that an invention might reasonably be expected to result from carrying out these duties. For example, where somebody is employed specifically on research and development work the individual would normally have no rights to any invention which he might develop. In practice, much will depend on the wording of the individual's job description and the terms and conditions of his employment.
2. When an employee has broad responsibilities and an obligation to further the interest of his employer's activities (eg directors and senior managers) it is assumed that any of their inventions would belong to the employer.

In all other circumstances inventions made by employees belong to them exclusively. The Act deals inter alia, under Sections 40, 41, 42 and 43, with various aspects of compensation for employee's inventions including procedures for claiming compensation from the Comptroller or Patents Court.

It is obviously advisable to seek professional advice when introducing suggestion schemes. In practice, it is important for employers to safeguard their own interests and ensure that suggestors are familiar with the rules of their company's scheme. The best solution is to print the rules on the back of the suggestion form to avoid any possible misunderstanding which may arise.

In the majority of cases where difficulties arise which could result in legal action, the root cause of the trouble can generally be traced back to inefficient administration and the failure to keep employees fully informed of the terms of the contract they entered into when they filled in the suggestion form.

The fact is not always appreciated that a suggestion is a contract and contains all three basic elements of a contract: offer, acceptance and adequate consideration. In 1975 in the United States the contractual implications of the suggestion were brought to the fore when two employees sued United Airlines for allegedly depriving them of what they considered to be their proper award for a tendered suggestion. United Airlines had given the two men $1,000 as an 'impetus award', this type of award being paid for an accepted suggestion which did not present a new idea in itself but merely speeded up action on a project or previous suggestion already submitted. The case was tried in a lower court and the two men awarded $368,049 in compensatory damages and $1,476,174 in punitive damages. On appeal to the California Court of Appeals in 1978 the decision of the lower court was reversed, the Appeal Court ruling that the suggestion did not qualify for a regular award under the provision of the United Airlines suggestion plan because it did not provide new or different ideas from those which had already been considered by the management and abandoned. The suggestion tendered merely provided an impetus towards reconsideration of the plans which had previously been considered but not,adopted. (If the suggestion had qualified for a regular award, the suggestors would have been entitled to receive a percentage of the savings generated by their idea as set out in the company's suggestion plan manual.)

The point that management need not pay awards for items already under consideration by management is a well established rule; however, the United Airlines case does, as the National Association of Suggestion Systems points out to its members, highlight the need for some additional legal guidelines in these areas.

American companies are now being advised to take a much closer look at the rules governing their schemes for any ambiguity or looseness of expression that might possibly be misinterpreted by suggestors.

Appendix D Suggestion Schemes Subject to Income Tax

Income tax will not be charged under Schedule E in respect of an award made by an employer to an employee under a staff suggestion scheme where the following conditions are satisfied:

(a) There is a formally constituted scheme under which suggestions are made and it is open to all employees on equal terms.

(b) The suggestion for which the award is made is outside the scope of the employee's normal duties. The test is whether, taking account of his or her experience, the employee could not reasonably have been expected to have put forward such a suggestion as part of the duties of his or her post. Where meetings of employees are held for the purpose of putting forward suggestions, they should be regarded as part of their duties and any consequential awards would not be within the terms of this concession.

(c) Awards other than encouragement awards (see paragraph (g)) are only made following a decision to implement the suggestion and are made directly to the employees concerned.

(d) The decision to make an award other than an encouragement award is based on the degree of improvement in efficiency and/or effectiveness likely to be achieved measured by reference to:
- the prospective financial benefits and the period over which they
  would accrue, and
- the importance of the subject matter having regard to the nature of the employer's business.

(e) The amount of an award does not exceed:
- 50 per cent of the expected financial benefit during the first year of implementation or
- 10 per cent of the expected net financial benefit over a period of up to 5 years, subject to an overriding maximum of £5,000. Where an award exceeds £5,000 the excess is not covered by this concession.

(f) Where a suggestion is put forward by more than one employee the award made under (e) above is divided between them on a reasonable basis.

(g) Any encouragement award is of £25 or less. An encouragement award is one which is made in respect of a suggestion which, though it will not be implemented, has some intrinsic merit and/or reflects meritorious effort on the part of the employee in making the suggestion.

This concession does not apply to any liability to income tax or capital gains tax on income or gains arising from the exploitation or disposal of rights in an invention devised by the employee, eg patent rights, know-how etc.

(This concession was announced in an Inland Revenue Press Release on 8 August 1986.)

Further Reading

Bayhylle, J E (1968) *Productivity Improvement in the Office*, Engineering Employers' Federation/Kogan Page, London.

Briscoe, G 'Employee Suggestion Schemes' *Management Services*, February 1976.

Evans, A (1982) *Practical Participation and Involvement 3. The Individual and the Job*, the Institute of Personnel Management, London.

Jago, A (1979) *Suggestion Schemes*, the Institute of Personnel Management, London.

Kilburn, D 'How suggestive workers nudge profits skywards' *Marketing Week*, 11 March 1988.

Leadbetter, C 'The value of suggestion schemes' *Financial Times*, 12 December 1986.

Leslie, N 'Suggestion schemes: the dos and don'ts of implementation *Financial Times*, 24 November 1981.

Macbeth, D 'Better brainpicking' *Industrial Society*, June 1982.

Marshall, G 'The factory suggestion box' *Industrial and Commercial Training*, March 1982.

Olsen, K 'Suggestion schemes seventies style' *Personnel Management*, April 1976.

Romano, S 'Bright ideas from the shopfloor pay off' *Works Management*, September 1986.

Root-Reed, M 'Bit of fun uncovers cost-cutting ideas' *Chief Executive*, October 1983.

'Shopfloor ideas prove participation pays' *Works Management*, July/August 1988.

Steward, J 'Rewards for employees who produce money-saving ideas' *Employee Bulletin and IR Digest*, April 1988.

Successful Suggestion Schemes, Industrial Society, London, 1988.

Suggestion Schemes Update 1988, Industrial Society, London, 1988.

Thornely, N 'Sharing ideas – the QED way' *Industrial Society*, June 1982.

Walker, A 'Why it's worth more than mere pennies for your thoughts' *Daily Mail*, April 1980.

Index